Growing Up In Frost

GROWING UP IN FROST

Memories From Small town America

Neil Palmer Kittlesen

Kirk House Publishers
Minneapolis, Minnesota

Growing Up In Frost
Memories From Small town America

Copyright © 2000 by Neil Palmer Kittlesen. All rights reserved
Editor: Barbara Walton Spradley
Format Design: Suzanne Kittlesen Tourtillott

First printing, August 2000.
Second printing, November 2000.
Third printing, August 2001.

Library of Congress Cataloging-in-Publication Data

Kittlesen, Neil Palmer, 1932-
  Growing up in Frost / Neil Palmer Kittlesen.
    p. cm.
  ISBN: 1-886513-60-0 (alk. paper)
   1. Kittlesen, Neil Palmer, 1932---Childhood and youth. 2. Frost (Minn.)--Biography. 3. Frost (Minn.)--Social life and customs--20th century. 4. City and town life---Minnesota--Frost. I. Title.

F614.F84 K58 2001
977.6'22--dc21
[B]
                                                                    2001038551

Kirk House Publishers, PO Box 39079, Minneapolis, MN 55439
Manufactured in the United States of America

For my wife, Bobbie
&
our children
&
our grandchildren
with love and gratitude

Table of Contents

Introduction 8
Acknowledgments 9
List of Illustrations 10
Map of Frost 12
Key to map of Frost 14
Where is Frost? 17
What is Frost? 18
Why Is Frost? 19
Pioneer Days 20
Steam Locomotives and Telegrams 21
The Great Depression 23
The Wedding 31
The Shivaree 32
Christmas Memories 33
The Great Armistice Day Blizzard 36
World War II 37
Main Street 41
Church 69

Number Please	74
Doc Hanson	76
School Days	81
Gymnasiums and Ball Fields	91
Dale Hanke	94
George Panzram	94
Bobby Griggs, The Music Man	98
The School Expands	102
Mom and Dad	104
Sitting Around the Radio	113
Flying	117
Outhouses and Halloween	118
Paper Boy	121
The News From Frost	123
People	124
The Ski Hill	127
Smaller than Frost	128
Epilogue	129

Introduction

This book began as a collection of memories about 14 years ago, when I got my first computer. For years I believed typing was a task too frustrating for me to ever do on a voluntary basis. Then I bought my first computer and discovered it was fun to write with a keyboard that makes corrections simple. What I had disliked was making corrections on a typewriter with erasers and many carbons.

This book is primarily a collection of memories of what it was like growing up in a small town during the 1930's and 1940's, the years of the Great Depression and World War II. The stories you are about to read are true. These are real people leading their lives in the midst of economic hardships and the tragedy of a second world war in their lifetimes.

Memories are selective and individual. Two people often remember the same event quite differently. Time blurs the details and sometimes the basic facts. While I have tried to be exact with names, places and events, I know that some will remember some things quite differently.

I feel fortunate to have grown up in a kind and caring community. Times were hard but the people were good. We had sad times and many happy occasions. Life is like that. A community where people care for each other is a special place and that's the Frost I remember with deep affection. I hope you will enjoy reading this book as much as I have enjoyed writing it. If you wish, please drop me a line or send me an e-mail. I would like to hear from you.

Neil Palmer Kittlesen
1081 Marie Avenue West
Mendota Heights MN 55118
email: neilpk@mac.com

Acknowledgements

When my wife, Barbara (Bobbie) Spradley, read my early efforts at recording memories she encouraged me to get serious and write them in book form. She is a successful author so it was more than personal and I began writing in earnest. Bobbie has also been the editor, artist, advisor and assistant for this book. The map of Frost as I remember it in 1940 is her work. She prepared much of the introductory material. Without her encouragement and suggestions my efforts would have never seen print. My love and thanks to Bobbie.

About two years ago on a visit to Frost, I traded stories with Larry Anderson while Bobbie enjoyed buying Scandinavian treasures at Sonja's Nordic World. Larry has been a wonderful friend and provider of stories, pictures, names, facts and figures and I thank him for his encouragement.

Thanks also to my niece, Suzanne Tourtillott. She is also an editor and author. She put my draft into book format and gave immeasurable assistance.

I am grateful to all who shared their memories and who helped fill in the blanks in my own recollections. Special thanks to those who took the time to find old photos and who trusted me with their valued keepsakes and stories: Bill Amundson, Jim Anderson, Sherwood Brekke, Arlen Erdahl, Mina Folven, Velma Griggs, Esther Gronfor, Linda Halverson, Connie Helgeson, Bill Isakson, Jim Johnson, Kristin Juliar, Jeff Kittlesen, Jim Kittlesen, Vivian Kittlesen, Leo Maland, Dorothy Nesheim, Ken Nesheim, Pat Oswald, Geraldine Shaw and Naomi Van Domelen.

Illustrations

Photos and news clippings courtesy of:

- (a) Jim Anderson
- (b) Larry Anderson
- (c) Velma Griggs
- (d) Connie Helgeson
- (e) Bill Isakson
- (f) Jeff Kittlesen
- (g) Jim Kittlesen
- (h) Neil Kittlesen
- (i) Mina Loge Folven
- (j) Leo Maland
- (k) Dorothy Nesheim
- (l) Naomi Van Domelen
- (m) Esther Anderson Gronfor

Naomi Kittlesen in sleigh and Neil Kittlesen (h) .... Front Cover
Peter Isakson and his dog in front of Ike's store (e) .... Page 18
Steam locomotive photographed in Spooner WI (h) 19
View of Frost in 1914 (g,k) 20
1917 REO touring car. 1947 parade (b,d,j) 21
Neil with Bill Isakson and the Frandle house (e,l) 25
Naomi Kittlesen's birthday party in 1942 (l) 29
Maytag Toy Racer. John Kittlesen at the wheel (h) 30
"Phooey on these drips" (h) 39
World War II Ration Book and coupons (h) 40
Blacksmiths at work 1914 (b,d,j) 42
Homecoming parade 1947: fire truck, blacksmith shop (b,d,j) 43
Homecoming parade 1947: beauty shop, Glen's Café (b,d,j) 44
Post Office, Gullord's Hardware and P J Erdal's store (e) 45
Willmert's Café, State Bank, Post Office, Ike's store (e) 46
Inez Isakson at the counter (e) 47
Clifford Kittlesen at Cashier's desk, Click at left (f) 49
State Bank of Frost. 1934 robbery (f) 50
Dad at his desk in 1939 (f) 50
Retiring and new directors at the State Bank (f) 51
Bank expansion and new Maland's Supply (f) 51
An early view of the railway depot in Frost (d,g) 58
Unloading sugar beets (d,g) 59
Ollie Savick, the depot and the new elevator complex (h) 61
Maland's Supply with Joseph J. Maland (b,d,j) 65

The Emerald Lutheran Church (d,g)	70
The Frost Lutheran Church (d,g)	71
Jim Anderson, Pastor Mosby, Neil Kittlesen (a)	73
Florence Loge on duty at Frost Telephone Central (i)	74
Newspaper clipping Minneapolis Tribune. Doc at age 70 (k)	79
Newspaper clipping Mankato Free Press. Doc in action (k)	80
The old wood frame school (d,g)	82
The old and new school buses (m)	82
New Frost school (m)	83
The new playground swing (l)	83
Esther Anderson (m)	84
Everyone had clean hands (m)	84
Grades 1, 2 & 3: 1939-40 (m)	84
Grades 1, 2 & 3: 1940-41 (m)	85
Who do you recognize (m)	85
Frost High School, 1937 with fire escape slide (h)	86
Frost basketball team 1937-38 (m)	87
Frost played 6 man football (m)	87
Pep Club 1937-38 (m)	88
Waitresses at 1953 junior–senior banquet (l)	90
Gymnasium with stage in raised position (h)	91
Orris Mortvedt and Gordy Gudahl. Jump ball (h)	94
Championship team seniors (h)	95
Newspaper clippings–Minneapolis Star and Tribune, Mankato Free Press, Faribault County Record and Bricelyn Sentinel (h)	96,97
Frost High School Band, 1951, Bobby Griggs at left (l)	98
Bobby Griggs Band post card (c)	99
Bobby Griggs, The Music Man (l)	101
Newspaper clipping–Bricelyn Sentinel (k)	103
Nell Kittlesen, 1955 (h)	106
Correspondence from State Bank of Frost files (h)	107,108
Clifford Kittlesen, Checkers Champion (h)	111
Helen and Naomi Kittlesen listening to our RCA radio (h)	113
1937 Stinson SR-10G (h)	117
The author at age 12 and today (h)	131

11

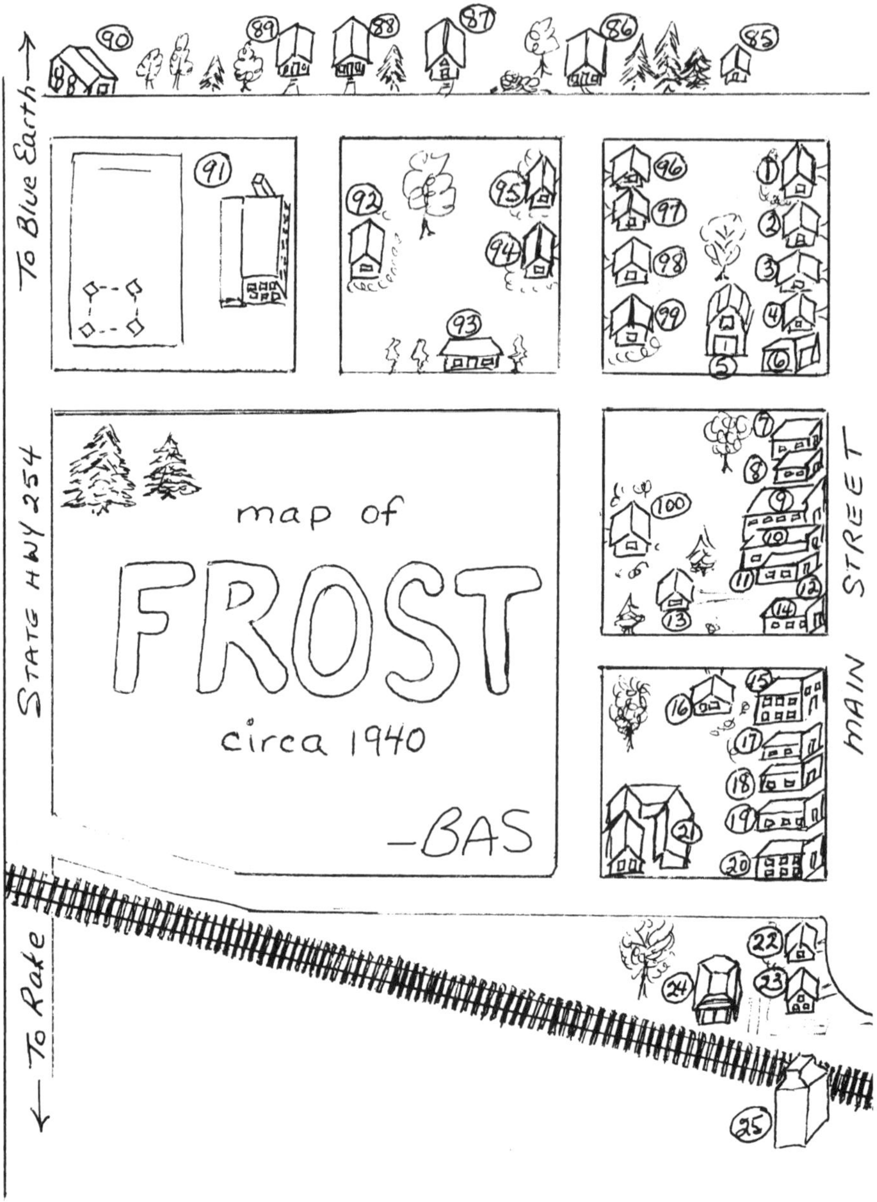
To Blue Earth
STATE HWY 254
To Rake
MAIN STREET
map of
FROST
circa 1940
—BAS

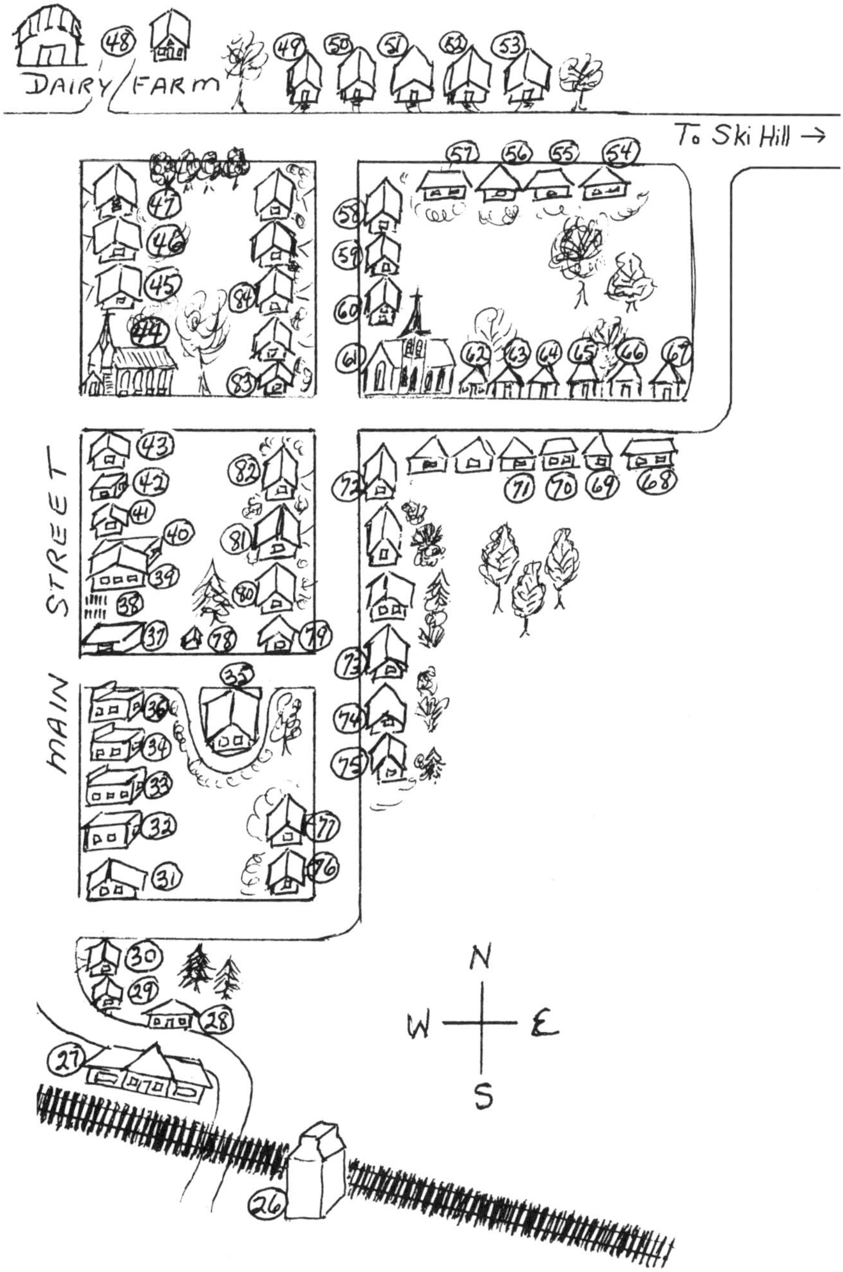

DAIRY FARM
To Ski Hill →
MAIN STREET
N
W
E
S
48
49
50
51
52
53
54
55
56
57
58
59
60
61
62
63
64
65
66
67
47
46
45
44
84
83
43
42
41
40
39
38
37
78
79
82
81
80
72
71
70
69
68
73
74
75
35
36
34
33
32
31
77
76
30
29
28
27
26

Key To Map Of Frost

1. Pete Peterson house
2. Ted Folken house
3. Doc Hanson's Clinic
4. Luddy and Mabel Erickson house
5. Livery Barn
6. Blacksmith Shop
7. Folken Restaurant
8. Margaret's Beauty Shop - Lubby and Margaret Roberts house
9. Ike's General Store - Ike and Inez Isakson house upstairs
10. Our Own Hardware
11. Post Office
12. Vacant lot used for band concerts and ice cream socials
13. Telephone Exchange - Belau/Midthun/Loge house
14. State Bank of Frost
15. Charlie Schroeder's Tavern
16. John Njoes house
17. Leonard's Café / Jonie's Café / Plumbing and Heating
18. Meat Market / Shorty Forthun's Cafe
19. Red and White Grocery
20. Produce - chickens live and dressed
21. Lumber Yard
22. Pearly and Mary Hegdal house
23. Clifford and Nell Kittlesen house
24. Beet dump
25. Grain elevator that burned
26. Site of new elevator complex
27. Railway Depot
28. Alfred Graue house
29. Ruby Brekke house
30. Nelmer Sabin house
31. Jensvold's Implements
32. Ted Nesheim Garage
33. Fire Station
34. Harness Shop / Henry Henderson Cafe
35. Creamery
36. Garage / warehouse
37. Maland's Supply
38. Free movie show lot
39. Doc Hanson's first office / Ed and Mildred Bartel house
40. Bergo Cafe / Ed Bartel's Barber Shop
41. Ted Gullord Office
42. Doc Johnson's Dental Clinic / City Hall
43. Doc Hanson's second office
44. Emerald Lutheran Church
45. Ollie Savick house
46. Dr. Lewis and Gert Hanson house
47. Martin Kallestad house
48. Maynard Helseth Dairy farm
49. Halvorson / Johnson house
50. George Carlson house

51. Johnson / Hegland house
52. Leo and Arlene Maland house
53. Henry Rygh house
54. Amund Brekke house
55. Chris and Tillie Anderson house
56. Leo and Arlene Maland's new house
57. Oscar and Jonette Maland house
58. Nelson house
59. Mrs. Frandle's house
60. Della Underdahl house
61. Frost Church
62. Thomas Nodland house
63. Henry Rygh's new house
64. Kittlesen's "middle" house
65. John Underdahl house
66. Juhl and Amanda Graue house
67. John Frandle house
68. Inkie and Clee Urness house
69. Nig Hanson house
70. John Nesje house
71. Emery Johnson house
72. Eddie and Cora Kallestad (Joe, Ernie and Mabel) house
73. Andrew Halvorson house
74. Obbie and Marion Johnson house
75. Ted and Hannah Nesheim house
76. Ralph and Eunice Amundson house
77. Charles Besendorf house
78. City Hall / beauty shop / REC
79. Ole Hattlestad house
80. George Panzram / Otis Honstad house
81. Alfred and Nellie Brandsoy house
82. Johnson house
83. Eddie Monson house
84. Earl and Al Sather house
85. Dale and Donna Hanke house
86. Juhl Willmert house
87. A.A. Erdahl house
88. Peter and Gert Thompson house
89. Lennis and Freda Quam house
90. Skelly Gas Station
91. School
92. R.M. Brekke house
93. Dr. Melly and Amy Johnson house
94. John and Malena Maland house
95. Joseph and Bertha Maland house
96. Eddie and Clarice Brekke house
97. Norton house
98. John and Anna Thompson / Martin and Winnie Shure house
99. Burton and Arlene Njoes house
100. Nonnie Midthun house

Where is Frost?

Where is Frost? If you grew up there, as I did, most of the people you met hadn't traveled very far, so you could say it's near Blue Earth. When I ventured a little farther and someone asked, "Where's Frost?" and then, Where's Blue Earth?" I would say it's between Fairmont and Albert Lea. When I went off to college and met people who had never heard of either Fairmont or Albert Lea, I would say Frost is south of Mankato. When I first got to the East Coast, I just said it's south of Minneapolis near the Iowa border.

When I arrived in France in the mid-fifties while in the army, my new French landlord asked me where I was from and I knew the above references wouldn't mean a thing, so with a bit of realism, I ventured "Frost is near Minneapolis". He gave me a look that made it clear he had never heard of Minneapolis, so I just said, it's in Minnesota. He shrugged again. The only other reference I could think of flashed in my mind and I said, "it's west of Chicago". He smiled and replied "Ah, *Chee-ca-go, gahng-stairs!*" (He had obviously seen too many gangster movies about Al Capone and others like him!) After that, I decided my response would be, "it's between Bricelyn and Elmore!" It was either that or "between New York and San Francisco!

Most of the people who hear the name, "Frost", automatically respond with "oh, that's up north, isn't it?" When they hear "between Bricelyn and Elmore", we are ready for a good conversation, especially when I see a blank look in their eyes and add, "well, that's on the east and west, if you look to the north and south, it's between Brush Creek and Rake"!

If Walter Mondale had succeeded Jimmy Carter as President of the United States, Elmore, his hometown, would have become as famous as Plains, Georgia and that would have been the end of my story!

What is Frost?

Frost is one of the thousands of small towns that sprang up in the early days as immigrants settled in the Midwest. It grew for about fifty or sixty years and peaked at a population of about three hundred twenty six.

When I was a kid, Frost was growing in population by about 25 people every decade. One of the kids would say something about how the town was changing and say, "I can remember when a dog could fall asleep in the middle of Main Street and be undisturbed all day. Now a car comes along every two or three hours and the dog has to wake up and move."

Peter Isakson and his dog in front of Ike's store

Another favorite story was telling someone that we could stand in the center of town and walk 2 blocks in any direction and be in the middle of a cornfield.

When the school closed (it merged with Blue Earth), businesses began closing and the town declined to the point where most of the homes in Frost had one elderly occupant, usually a widow, and many of the homes were vacant. There was no market to sell my Dad's house in the sixties and seventies with the result that it was on the market for sixteen years. We finally had to auction it off for less than the price of an older used car. In the 1980's, there must have been more houses on the market than not. Now, Frost is growing again. It has become a bedroom community with workers commuting to Blue Earth, Wells, Albert Lea, Fairmont, Mankato and a number of long distance truckers who find it convenient to live near the junction of interstate highways 35 and 90. The town is looking good again. Many of the homes have new additions and have been remodeled with fresh coats of paint. Frost now has a population of about two hundred fifty one.

Why Is Frost?

The Chicago Northwestern Railroad expanded in 1899, running new track in a northwesterly direction from Mason City through north central Iowa into southern Minnesota connecting with an east-west line in Lamberton.

The steam locomotives needed to add water to their boilers every eight miles, so the railway built stations at eight mile intervals and towns were developed around each station to provide for the pick up and delivery of goods to the settlers homesteading new lands. This spacing of stations allowed farmers to come to the station by horse and wagon and return home the same day. So that's the answer to "why?" and helps explain why small towns need a new reason for being or they die off unless, of course, steam locomotives make a comeback!

Pioneer Days

One of the small towns that developed along the new railroad was Frost, Minnesota, named for Charles S. Frost, the Chicago architect who designed the new railway depots.

View of Frost in 1914, looking north to main street, old school at far left

Frost soon developed into a thriving community with two hotels, a general store, a grocery store, drug store, an opera house, two millinery shops (ladies' hats were in fashion then), two lumber yards, a sawmill, brick and tile plant, a livery barn and dray line (ask your grandfather what that was all about), meat market, four blacksmith shops, a harness shop, hardware store, a farm implement store, creamery, barber shop, four restaurants, two grain elevators, several auto repair garages and gas stations, post office, a doctor and a dentist and two Lutheran Churches. Two long-forgotten automobile models, the Brush and the Allen, had dealerships in Frost and someone even converted a rubber-tired buggy into an automobile at one of the blacksmith shops. The blacksmith used a rope drive to connect the engine to the wheels.

1917 REO touring car, blacksmith shop, livery barn. 1947 parade

Steam Locomotives and Telegrams

The train depot was one of the most active places in town and vital to its life and economy. Goods of all kinds arrived in Frost by train and were then delivered to businesses and individuals. Telegrams brought news of deaths and other vital information. They must have brought good news also, but I can only remember the sad ones, especially the telegrams during World War II. One told us of the death of my Canadian cousin, Vernon Symons, when his parachute failed to open during a training exercise and another one told us that my cousin, Jimmy Marjach, was killed by an enemy sniper during the invasion of Leyte Island in the Phillipines. The telegram that I remember most vividly was delivered verbally. My Grandfather Charlie Palmer was seriously ill at age 80. Mother and Dad had driven to northern Minnesota to be with him at what appeared to be the end of his life. Ollie Savick walked to our house to tell my brother Jim and me that he had just received a telegram from my parents. Our grandfather had just died. I never asked whether the telegram was addressed to him asking him to give us the news or whether he just knew that he should tell us the news in person rather than handing us a sealed telegram.

Ollie Savick was the depot agent and the telegrapher,

the freight agent, the passenger ticket agent and handler of all the other duties for the railway. He was everyone's friend and so the depot was a magnet for all the kids in town. We were always happy to help him get the incoming freight boxes ready for delivery, or collect freight charges from the merchants or do any other useful chores. The railway was our main connection to the rest of the world so it was an exciting place to hang out.

One fourth of July, in about 1942, one of the kids was wandering about town throwing firecrackers wherever he could cause a little mischief, scaring animals and in general raising Cain. My friend, Sherwood Brekke, began following him out of curiosity probably. He happened to see the kid put a firecracker in a hole in the depot outer wall. Sure enough, the firecracker dropped down inside the wall and started a fire. Sherwood put in the alarm and soon the firemen were hard at work trying to extinguish the blaze. It was starting to get out of hand when a train approached Frost. The fire hoses were stretched across the track and someone had to signal the train to make an unscheduled stop or the locomotive would have severed the fire hoses. Ollie was frantic and urged everyone to redouble their efforts, telling them; "if this depot burns to the ground, the railroad will never build us a new one". Fortunately, they succeeded in putting out the blaze. The charred timbers in the freight house were painted over but the evidence of the fire remained as long as the depot did.

Three or four men called the "section crew" maintained the tracks and kept them in good repair. They had a small vehicle that must have been gas powered that rolled along the tracks.

One day the freight train engineer asked a group of us kids (who were all shirtless and barefoot) about the purpose of our belly buttons. We didn't have a clue so he told us, "it's where you put salt when you eat celery in bed".

Cinders from the coal burning locomotives were used to line the track bed and also used to pave the street and a footpath for a block north of the depot (past our house). Walking on cinders with bare feet was a challenge; I guess we all developed some awesome calluses.

We took pride in being able to walk the rails without falling off. On a good day we could walk the train tracks all the way to Marna (a one-time town that was then only a grain elevator next to the tracks) and we put pennies on the track to see how the train flattened them into large thin ovals.

I remember the lonesome whistle of the steam locomotives and train rides for 10 cents to Blue Earth (or Fairmont for a little more). The train was our link to the outside world and those short trips were special adventures.

The Great Depression

My parents moved to Frost in 1930 when the depression was affecting everyone and everything. My father had been a banker in northern Minnesota. However, in 1930, the owner of the State Bank of Frost persuaded Dad that he was the right person to steer the bank through turbulent waters. Dad was a banker for fifty years. His banking career took him through the great depression, World War II and all that followed, until his retirement as president due to ill health in 1958 and his second retirement a year before he died in 1964.

Dad never forgave Roosevelt for closing all the banks in the United States for a few days after taking over the Presidency in 1933. Roosevelt believed that action was necessary to restore trust in a troubled banking industry, but Dad's bank was sound and he believed it was wrong to close the good banks with the bad ones. Dad considered it to be a personal insult.

I remember Dad telling me that there was one good job in a small town bank and that was to own it. He never was the owner. He did own 20% of the stock by the time of his first retirement, but that's not enough to be the owner! His comment helped persuade me to seek a different career.

I was born on November 25, 1932 at Northwestern Hospital in Minneapolis. Doc Hanson had just arrived in Frost the year before but the town never did have a hospital. In those days, there were no paved roads in Frost nor were they paved leading into and out of Frost or to the nearest hospital. The roads were bad even in the best times of the year and 30 miles on bad roads in late November didn't seem like the best way to have a baby. Dad's sister, my Aunt Dena, lived in Minneapolis, within a few blocks of Northwestern Hospital, so Mother went to stay with her until I was ready to make my appearance.

US Highway 16 was not paved between Albert Lea and Blue Earth until sometime in the 1930's. I don't remember exactly when but I was old enough to remember that we used a detour to get to Blue Earth during the construction and that it was a big deal when the newly paved highway re-opened. We didn't have any paved roads coming into town until State Highway 254 from US 16 to the Iowa border was paved in the early 1950's.

As I remember it, houses always carried the name of the family who had lived there previously, not the name of the current tenants. My family lived in the Njoes house when I was born. It was conveniently located across the street and down the block behind the bank. One of my earliest memories is riding in a wagon, pulled by my brother John. We had just moved from the Njoes house to the Frandle house on the corner at the east edge of town. Mrs. Njoes, who had moved back into their house, invited us to pick apples from the tree that had been ours and John was selected to gather the crop. He took me along for company and hopefully to get a little help but I doubt that I was old enough to do more than pick up a few apples that had fallen to the ground.

Neil with Bill Isakson and the Frandle house

The Frandle house had lots of special features for a small boy to appreciate and remember. We had a real bathroom with running water from a cistern that collected the rain as it ran off the roof. A section of the basement was walled off to form the cistern. The wall came just short of the ceiling and I marvelled to think about all the water that was stored just over that wall. The cistern supplied us with water for bathing, washing clothes and flushing the toilet. We got our drinking water from a pump in the back yard using a pail and dipper that sat on the kitchen counter. I remember pumping that pail full of water many times and the entire family drinking from that same dipper.

The basement of the Frandle house also had a room that was just right for a pool table. My brothers, John and Click, bought a used pool table along with several friends as partners. We had the best (and probably the only) place for the table, so I learned to shoot pool in my own basement at a very early age! We also had an unfinished attic—just right for a play area for imaginative kids!

Click and some of his friends owned an old Model T Ford. He gave us a ride to school in it many times, but it rarely started without a push. We would push it a block to the church corner and then another block down the hill to Obbie and Marion Johnson's house hoping that the hill would be enough to get it started. If the Model T still didn't start, we pushed it up the next hill to and around the creamery. That way we had the hill back down the creamery driveway to get it started. As I remember that always worked and then we would jump in the moving Model T to ride three and a half blocks to school. Riding in the car was so exciting for us that it didn't matter that the school was only four blocks away from home.

My brother Click was good with money. To be able to own shares of a pool table and a car while he was still in high school, in the middle of the great depression, took a special talent that he developed early in life. When he was very young, he always seemed to have money on Sundays. My parents were curious and asked him where he got it. Click replied, "They pass it out in Sunday school"! I guess it was no surprise that he turned out to be a successful banker!

Our neighbors next door were Juhl and Amanda Graue. Amanda's mother lived with them. She had been in poor health for many years and seemed to need a "hypo" on a regular basis. She was also deaf and had an ear trumpet. That was an interesting type of hearing aid. It had an earpiece, a long hollow tube and a bell shaped end for her visitors to speak into. Amanda was a very good cook and always had treats for me when I visited. One of my favorites was a cookie known as a kringla. I had given up ever enjoying that taste again until I saw Linda Halverson's kringla story on the Frost web site. Her sister, Pat Oswald, graciously furnished the recipe for me and for you to enjoy:

Kringla
1 egg	1 cup sugar
1 cup sour cream or milk	1 teaspoon baking soda
1 teaspoon vanilla	1 teaspoon baking powder
butter the size of a large egg	a pinch of salt
flour enough to roll, but not too much	

Beat eggs, sugar and vanilla together. Mix sour cream and soda and add to egg mixture. Sift dry ingredients and add to mixture. Dough is easier to work with if made and refrigerated overnight. Working with a small amount at a time, roll rope fashion on a floured board, cut into about 8" strips and fold into knots or figure 8. Bake on ungreased pan about 8 minutes at 350 or until light brown and done to the touch.

Recipe from the kitchen of Elvina Midthun, courtesy of her granddaughter Patricia Amundson Oswald who adds: "With my mother's help, we came up with 1/4 cup of butter and about 3 cups of flour. I finally learned to roll kringla after working with playdough with my kids".

In our own family discussions about this treat, I discovered that my sister-in-law, Vivian Kittlesen, also has a kringla recipe! So now I can share hers with you too:

Kringla

1 cup sour cream	1 egg
1 teaspoon baking powder	4 cups flour
1 teaspoon baking soda	1 cup buttermilk
dash of salt and nutmeg	1 cup sugar
1 rounded tablespoon butter	1 teaspoon vanilla

Mix all together and chill overnight. Using small amounts of dough on floured board, pat with flour, roll into a long roll and form into figure 8's on cookie sheet. Bake in 350 oven 8–10 minutes.

Other variations we found include adding a dash of nutmeg, anise or cardamom seed. If you decide to try baking kringla, I would be happy to taste your results!

We were renting the Frandle house and finally had a chance to buy it for $3,500. Unfortunately, the FHA would not approve a mortgage. I guess they didn't think it was worth that much! It was an ideal house for our family, but since he couldn't sell it, Johnnie Frandle decided to move into it with his family and remodel it. So we moved again. This time we moved three houses west to what we called "the house in the middle of the block" and lived only in the downstairs portion of the house. Many years later I ran into our upstairs neighbor who told me a wonderful story about that time. He and his wife were newlyweds and their bedroom was directly above my parents' bedroom. One night the slats on their bed broke and crashed loudly to the floor. He was embarrassed to think about seeing my Dad the next day so did his best to avoid him. But as luck would have it, they did run into each other. He said my Dad, a serious man, didn't say a word but smiled and winked at him!

Our neighbor, John Underdahl, had been blinded by a dynamite explosion. I would walk with him and talk with him often. My brother-in-law, Kenny, remembers the time I was walking with John around town and stopped at the shop where he and his Dad were working. John told them, "This Kittlesen boy is a good boy. He walks me around town and I gave him a nickel." Then I said "Yea, and he's going to give me another nickel, aren't you, John?" John didn't say a word and I don't recall getting another nickel. Another idea that went nowhere!

John's daughter, Clara and her husband, Regg Johnson, would come to visit every year from California in a new Buick, as I remember. A new Buick every year in the middle of the depression! I was impressed! But the story gets better; Regg would call out to the first kid he saw, usually me, "Round up all the kids you can find and meet me at Folken's for ice cream". I thought he was the richest and most generous man in the world. I might find 20 kids and at 5 cents for an ice cream cone, that meant he would spend a whole dollar on a bunch of kids!

One of the memories I had trouble believing was true was reinforced when I asked my sister for help with this project. Naomi asked me, "Did lightning really strike between a group of us as we stood outside John Underdahl's house with Don Irving?" Yes, it did! We were all within inches of a direct hit but none of us was injured at all.

Naomi Kittlesen's birthday party in 1942

We were able to buy a house a year or two later. Dad bought the last house on the south end of Main Street. It needed a lot of work so Mother and Dad spent many hours remodeling and painting to make it more livable. It was the first house that I remember where our bedrooms were upstairs and it got pretty hot up there in the summer time. Air conditioning was rare in those days but Dad was inventive. He rigged up a device that sprayed water on a piece of sheet metal that he mounted at the point where the cold air return entered the furnace. It made the house a lot more comfortable but it did add more humidity than necessary or desirable! Some years later, he bought a window air conditioner which worked much better!

Washing clothes was not a simple task in those days. It meant pumping soft rainwater from the cistern into a pail that, in turn, was emptied into a copper double boiler. It took many pails full to fill the boiler. Then the kerosene burners were lit under the boiler and the water was heated and ladled from the boiler into the Maytag wringer washing machine and the rinse tubs. I remember hanging the sheets on the line. The sun dried them in the summer and they would freeze dry in the winter resulting in a clean-smelling wash all year-round. When we heard the whistle of the coal-burning steam locomotive, we had to run outside to bring them in even if they were wet. We had to rescue the freshly washed clothes from being covered by engine smoke that was loaded with black coal soot. Otherwise, it meant they would have to be washed again.

We were lucky to have an electric Maytag. People without electricity, and there were many of them including my grandparents, had gasoline powered washing machines that had to be kept out on a porch to protect the family from the gas fumes. After the wash had been rinsed and run through the wringer, it was put in a large basket and carried out to be hung on the clothesline. The baskets were wicker, not plastic, so they were heavy even when empty. When full of wet clothes, they were really heavy! I guess the folks with gasoline-powered washers had one advantage, they had a much shorter distance to carry the wash to the clothesline! You may think that's why many continued to use their gasoline-powered washing machines after electricity arrived at their place. The real reason was that no one bought anything new as long as they could still repair the old one to keep it working! It must have been miserable to stand outdoors pulling wet clothes out of the washing machine to run them through the wringer into rinse water and again through the wringer into the basket and then pin them to the clothesline in the middle of the winter!

Maytag Toy Racer.
John Kittlesen at the wheel

Dad was a master at building a coal fire in the furnace that lasted all through a cold winter night. He stoked up the coals until they were almost white-hot, then banked the fire with ashes until only a small hole remained in the center so that the fire burned all night without burning itself out. Thanks to his skill we woke up fairly warm rather than freezing cold!

When I was a senior in high school, I had a bad experience with that furnace. I had spread newspapers all over the floor to paint something. When I was done, I grabbed all the papers, intending to put them in the furnace. The problem was as I threw the wadded-up newspapers into the furnace, my new gold class ring slipped off and went with the paper into the blazing fire! Worse yet, I wasn't used to having a ring on my finger and didn't even notice what I had done for an hour or more. When I sifted through the coals, I sadly found the blackened remains of my gold ring. Fortunately, I was able to send it back to Jostens and they recast the ring. I don't think they even charged me for it!

My other memories of the years of the great depression are pretty dim. I was a little boy growing up in a small town. Everyone else was poor too so how was I to know it could be any different? If we didn't already have something, we knew we really didn't *need* it even though we very much *wanted* it. We fixed things that broke and never threw anything away unless it was hopelessly broken.

Dad was a fanatic about keeping everything because "it might come in handy someday". I remember taking some old junk to the garbage can with Mother and watching her carefully hide the junk under some "real" garbage. I asked her why. With her ever-present smile, Mom said that Dad would just bring the junk back into the house if he saw it in the garbage can! That mentality still affects me today. It's still hard to throw anything away but I've also worn a smile most of my life as my Mother did for all of hers.

The Wedding

I remember my sister's wedding in that house on the corner. I was only three years and three months old, so it probably is my earliest memory. Dorothy married Kenneth

Nesheim. I couldn't understand why Dorothy wouldn't be living with the family any more. My mother explained that she would now live with Kenny. I asked Mom, "Why doesn't Kenny take Click?" No one in the family remembers Mom's answer, but apparently neither Kenny nor Click, nor Dorothy for that matter, thought very much of my suggestion!

Kenny was kind to me in spite of that foolish idea. One day he was visiting with my Dad in our living room. I was behind Dad so he couldn't see me playing with Kenny's homburg hat. I was pushing the top in and out, crushing and pummeling was probably more like it, and Kenny wanted to clobber me. He knew that Dad would punish me worse than he would so he just gritted his teeth and hoped that I wouldn't cause permanent damage to his fine hat! I only heard that story recently. I was probably about three years old and even though I remember their wedding, I can't remember smashing Ken's hat, but when he told me the story, I told him that I owed him for that favor!

Dorothy remembers that Frost was completely snow-bound in February of 1936, the week that she and Ken were married. Some of the snowdrifts were as high as telephone wires. Because of unplowed roads, Dorothy and Ken were unable to get to the courthouse to get their wedding license and there was a five-day waiting period in those days. The judge waived the requirement for them and the wedding went on as planned on Valentine's Day.

The Shivaree

It was customary in those days to surprise newlyweds on their wedding night with a shivaree. I remember that the whole town (almost) gathered quietly in the dark surrounding the newlyweds' darkened house late in the evening. At a signal, everyone starting making a terrible racket, banging on pots and pans and anything else that made lots of noise. We kept at it until the newlyweds reluctantly turned on their lights and came to the door. Then everyone cheered and the groom was expected to provide beer for the adults and pop for the kids and the bride was expected to provide food for everyone. The newlyweds always just happened to have the snacks and drinks, so I guess it was no surprise.

Not knowing a shivaree was a traditional celebration it seemed to me to be a dirty trick to play on newlyweds on their wedding night. But everyone seemed to enjoy it and expect it. It was also a lot more fun than the reception held in the church basement right after the wedding where all anyone got was coffee, mints and a few mixed nuts to go with a small piece of wedding cake. I did a little research on the subject and found that shivaree is an Americanized spelling and pronunciation of charivari, a seven hundred year old French tradition with as many variations as the communities that looked for an excuse for a celebration. I've heard since of other ways to celebrate a shivaree but this is the way we did it in Frost.

Christmas Memories

Our Christmas tree lights were shaped like candles and bubbled. We also had some that glowed in pastel colors (they were round globes and looked like ornaments and were fluorescent I think). I also remember the old type tree lights that would all go out if one bulb burned out so you had to test every bulb on the string until you found the one that was burned out. If two or more burned out at the same time, it was close to impossible to get the right combination to make it light up again. Today, you could just replace all the bulbs with new ones or more likely you would just buy a whole new string. But in the depression years no one would think of throwing away even one good bulb and we rarely had more than a few extras. No, I am not old enough to remember anyone using real candles on their Christmas tree.

On Christmas Eve we each got one present from the folks, often clothing, and then a gift the next morning from Santa. One year I got a flashlight and thought to myself it was smart to believe in Santa so you could get two gifts!

I remember the year my nephew, Joey Nesheim, received an electric train for Christmas. We all joined in to set it up on the dining room table with newspapers under the tracks to protect the table. When we were ready for the next meal, the train had to be disassembled so we could use the table for dinner—how many times did we set it up, take it down and set it up again?

I longed for an electric train but was never that lucky. Years later, in Milwaukee, a co-worker gave me his old electric train and I gave it to my son Dave for Christmas. Now I have a cast iron reproduction of a steam passenger train to put at the base of the Christmas tree. It gave me such a good warm glow that now we have it on a shelf at our cabin all year round!

Church dinners were a tradition throughout the year and especially at Christmas. The first time I ever had oyster stew was at a church supper so I didn't see how it was made. I thought that the crackers were transformed into an entirely different kind of taste when they were soaked in the milk and sank to the bottom of the bowl. I discovered that I was tasting oysters for the first time.

Mostly I remember the good and abundant food with all of us together for a wonderfully good time. Mom would make sweet potatoes with marshmallows melted on top and lots of other goodies. While Dad and Milt played checkers, Mom and Gustie Jenkins made great candies. A pecan log roll was my favorite and I've never been able to find one that tasted that good since. Mom's divinity, chocolate covered coconut candies, and lots of other goodies were out of this world. I'm drooling just thinking about all that good stuff! Fortunately my sister, Naomi, kept Mom's divinity recipe:

Divinity
2 1/2 cup sugar
1/4 teaspoon salt
3/4 cup candied cherries
2/3 cup light corn syrup
2 egg whites, stiffly beaten
1/2 cup nut meats
1/2 cup water
1/2 teaspoon vanilla for coloring, if desired

In saucepan, cook sugar, syrup, water & salt, stirring until sugar is dissolved. Then cook, without stirring, to brittle stage. Slowly blend into egg whites. Shape into rolls & coat as directed in next recipe:

Caramel coating for divinity roll
2/3 cup sugar
1 1/4 cup cream
1 tablespoon vanilla
1/2 cup light corn syrup
a pinch of salt
chopped pecans spread on wax paper

Prepare 1 recipe divinity & form into logs. Bring sugar, syrup, cream & salt to a boil then slowly cook to a medium hard ball stage. Add vanilla. Set pan in hot water to prevent hardening. Hold divinity roll between two forks and dip into caramel mixture, coating well. Quickly drop roll into chopped nuts & coat completely. Press nuts into roll. Dip marshmallows in extra caramel & coat with nuts for an extra treat

Chocolate caramel coating for divinity roll
1 cup white sugar
1/2 cup cream
3 squares baking chocolate
1/2 cup brown sugar
1 cup milk
1 tablespoon vanilla,
1/2 cup light corn syrup
1/4 cup butter

Prepare using directions for caramel coating listed above.

Recipes from the kitchen of Nell Kittlesen

The Great Armistice Day Blizzard

November 11, 1940, dawned a mild, beautiful day, especially for early November. There were no warnings of any changes expected in the weather. About 10 that morning the wind began to blow and the snow began falling; in just a few moments it was apparent that a major storm was developing. The school was closed so that everyone could return to their homes as quickly as possible.

Mary Lee and Billy Isakson's dad was outside the school ready to drive his kids home. My brother, Jim, and I and as many others who could, squeezed into Ike's car. As he started slowly towards Main Street the visibility vanished and within two blocks he was asking if anyone could see anything. I caught a glimpse of a corner of the livery barn and called it out to Ike who thanked me because that meant we were within a few yards of Main Street. We turned the corner, stopped in front of Ike's store and all got out of the car.

In the blinding snow Jim and I set out on foot for the remaining two blocks to our house. We did alright until we got to the neighbors, the Graue's. My eyes were completely covered with snow and I couldn't see across the yard to our house. I pressed my face against Graue's side door and literally dug the snow from my eyes so that I could make it the last few feet to our home. With my delay, Jim arrived home alone and Mom asked him where I was. Sheepishly, he said he didn't know and Mom told him to go back out and find me. He did and brought me home safely.

There were many rescue stories about that day. I remember one in particular. Glen (Tommy) Thompson and his sister, Edna, decided to stay with friends in town rather than chance the trip to their farm but Edna was a diabetic and needed her insulin and had none or not enough with her. Tommy fearlessly set out and walked the two miles home in the blinding storm to get her insulin and then turned right around and walked the two miles back to town. He was acclaimed a hero and rightly so. He risked his own life to save his sister and thought nothing of the risk he took in doing so!

A few years later, someone in Frost put together a strange contraption. It had tracks on the back (like a caterpillar) and skis on the front. It had the frame and engine of an old car or truck and a homemade box for a body that had room for several people and necessary supplies. It was built to provide safe rescue for anyone caught in a future storm. It may very well have been the world's first snowmobile!

World War II

I remember clearly hearing the news on the radio that Sunday morning of December 7, 1941. The Japanese had bombed Pearl Harbor and we were at war.

A year or so earlier all the young men had been required to register for selective service. The first from Frost to be drafted into the army was Morrie Maland, if I remember correctly. It didn't seem likely at that point that war would actually come and I remember someone saying; "Morrie stuck his head out the window and got caught in the draft!"

After Pearl Harbor was attacked, everything changed. My brother John tried to enlist in the Army Air Corps (the Air Force didn't become a separate service until later). John failed the eye exam, came home and ate carrots by the ton and failed it again. But that time he hung around the exam room long enough to memorize the chart. The next time, he passed the exam!

John was a flight engineer and top turret gun operator on a B-25 Mitchell bomber, based in England with the 8th Air Corps. He told the family that his duties were mostly on the ground, because he didn't want them to worry about him. Many years later he was able to answer my direct question about his actual duties. He had flown 25 combat missions over Germany. The official policy then was to relieve men from combat flights after 25 missions, figuring that they had cheated death long enough.

My brother Click also enlisted in the Army Air Corps but he too was rejected. In his case, the problem was his slight build. He went on a weight gain diet, eating bananas and drinking malted milks and when he reached his weight goal, the air corps doctors discovered he was color blind to a slight degree. That disqualified him for the Air Corps but the Army was glad to take him. He was assigned to the medics doing paper work and was sent to the South Pacific. There he was assigned to an island hospital in the New Hebrides.

On free days Click enjoyed floating in the bay on an air mattress. One day while he was relaxing in the water, the tide went out suddenly and he was swept out to sea amidst the warships. He tried desperately to paddle with his hands but was unable to make any progress against the big waves. He was sure he was doomed to either drown or be crushed by one of the large ships. After many hours, the tide changed again and took him back him to the bay. He was thrown up on the shore safe and sound but quite a distance from his station. He found his way back to the hospital area and, as far as we know, never tried that form of relaxation again! His good friend and neighbor from Frost, DeVere Brekke, was in the Navy during the war and made a stop in the New Hebrides. Unfortunately, neither knew the other was there or they could have had a good visit together.

Click saw Japanese fighter planes occasionally, but maybe he thought it was too safe a place to be. Maybe it was seeing all the wounded men in the hospital or that he felt he wasn't doing his share. So he volunteered for the infantry and was on orders to go to the Philippine Islands for further training. While he was waiting to go, the atomic bombs were dropped on Hiroshima and Nagasaki. The war was over!

It's hard for me to second-guess the wisdom of using

atomic bombs to end the war. The alternative would surely have been an invasion of Japan with an even greater cost in lives, American and Japanese. And my brother Click would have been part of the invading army.

Everyone in America with a son in the military had a service flag in their front window. The flags had a blue star on a white background with a red border. If their son was killed in action, the flag had a gold star. Most of the houses in Frost had one or more service flags in the window—one for each son in the service. We were lucky to have blue stars on our two flags.

I suppose that I was more aware of what went on during the war than most kids my age as a result of having brothers involved in Europe and in the Pacific. Life at home was different and I suppose many at home suffered hardships but compared to the soldiers, sailors and airmen who fought the battles, our inconveniences were minor.

I made two scrapbooks of newspaper and magazine clippings of the news of the war. I still have both of them. One of the clippings is a magazine advertisement with caricatures of Hitler, Tojo, and Mussolini and the words: "Uncle Sam has far more power for war production than all these three together!" My boyish scrawl is still visible where I had x'd out the three faces and written: "Phooey On These Drips". I still think that was a good statement for a ten year old kid.

Gasoline and food and almost everything that we could buy were rationed. Every adult and child had ration coupons that limited food items we could buy. Some items like bananas and coffee were rare treats because they often were just not available. Even then, we had a world economy and the supply lines were disrupted by the war. South Pacific islands were captured by the Japanese, merchant marine ships were needed for the war effort, the list went on and on.

Drivers had a decal on their windshield to indicate whether their car was used for business or pleasure. I guess you got more ration coupons if you needed your car for business reasons. To conserve gasoline, the highway speed limit was reduced to 35 miles per hour. Most drivers obeyed the limit. Some probably didn't but my Dad believed it was our responsibility to follow the law. And he did! Not 36 or 37 mph even; we went 35 no matter how long it took to get to our destination. When we went to visit Grandma and Grandpa in northern Minnesota, it took about 12 hours to make the 325-mile trip. Rubber was in very short supply and so everyone had to take special care to make their tires last as long as possible.

Many of those who fought the war and lived though it carried unspoken burdens for the rest of their lives. Paul Underdahl was a marine and was part of the invasion of Saipan and as far as I know, he never talked about it with anyone. Al Fenske lost an eye during a battle somewhere in the Pacific. My Dad and I saw Al just after he returned home. Dad asked him very kindly how he was doing. I don't remember Al's response, but I'll never forget Dad curse the war and the people who caused so much human suffering. It's the only time I remember hearing Dad swear.

Main Street

The last time I visited Frost most of the old stores, shops and restaurants were gone from Main Street, replaced by nice green lawns. It looked better than seeing old, decaying buildings.

When I was growing up, the sights and sounds along Main Street became embedded in my memory like a rancher's branding iron. There were the neighing of horses as they pulled heavy wagons, chugging Model T's and later newer cars that scattered chickens who ran squawking and crowing for safety, dogs barking or sleeping in the sun, and lots of people. On Saturday nights the farmers came to town dressed up in their best bib overalls (ones that were never used for work) with clean plaid shirts and ties. They would sit on the benches in front of the stores and swap stories while their wives shopped for groceries and dry goods for the next week while their kids were at the free show, one of my favorite memories of Frost. I will describe that more fully a little later.

Main Street was about four blocks long, if you were willing to include everything. In the 30's and 40's, when I was growing up, you could take a walk up and down Main Street, starting at the north end and on the west side of the street, and here's what you would see.

In block one; the corner two-story frame house was the home of Mr. and Mrs. Pete Peterson. He was a retired veterinarian. The next house was the home of Amelia Halvorson, then Ted Folken, then Webbie and Dorothy Nesheim and then Gay and Dorothy Anderson. Next was a vacant lot for many years that later became the site of Doc Hanson's new medical clinic.

After that came Ludwig (Luddy) and Mabel Erickson's

place. Luddy operated a truck line delivering freight and other merchandise. He stored his trucks in the livery barn behind his house. In the early days, the livery barn had been built for horses and wagons. Martin Kallestad bought the livery business in 1914. Martin was an entrepreneur. In addition to hauling goods to and from the railway depot and providing a place to board and rent horses, he had a horse drawn open buggy that he used as a taxi to take people around the Frost area and to neighboring towns. I remember when the livery barn was torn down. It had outlived its usefulness, but it was sad to see it go.

The corner building was the blacksmith shop operated by Karl Eichler. It was a fascinating place for me as a youngster. I can still smell the white-hot forge. Karl would pump the bellows until the coals were as hot as possible and then grasp a plowshare with huge tongs and place it in the fire until it glowed a translucent red. He would then hammer the blade until the nicks and breaks were smoothed out and the blade had a sharp edge again. Next he would drop the plowshare into a vat of water to temper and cool it off so he could remount it. I can still hear the sizzle and see the steam from the sudden impact of the hot metal in the cool water.

I remember another blacksmith at that same shop who always had a plug of chewing tobacco in his cheek. Once he was working on a farm wagon in front of the shop and paused thoughtfully and then walked into the shop and spit his tobacco on the shop floor!

Blacksmiths at work, 1914

Apparently, he thought that better than spitting on the clean ground! Well, the inside of a blacksmith shop was always dirty from the coal and metal shavings and other junk.

Homecoming Parade 1947: Neil and Dale Chilson on back of fire truck, Kerm and Ken Northwick sitting on top of truck at top right

    The second block began with Folken's Restaurant, home of the ice cream shop and family style Sunday dinners. The owner, Ted Folken, and his family lived in the back of the building behind the restaurant. They served Sunday dinners family style at a large table. All the food was passed around the table and everyone was welcome to as much food as they wanted including second and third helpings. Folkens was the gathering place for kids and grownups. The ice cream cones were always generous and were only a nickel! They had a great candy counter with all kinds of candy served in bulk or packaged. I remember red hots, jawbreakers, orange slices, licorice and candy bars that only cost five cents each.

After the war, Glen Nesheim ran the café for a few years before moving into the grocery business at the other end of Main Street.

Homecoming parade 1947. beauty shop, barber shop and Glen's Cafe

Before Folkens took over, it was Oscar Severtson's Café. He was not in the best of health and needed to take a nap every day or at least get a rest break. He used a room just off the dining area for this purpose and put a sign on the door that read, "Oscar's Rest Room". Everyone in town understood this but it became a problem for "out-of-towners". They saw the sign and assumed it meant what you and I would think today. When they opened the door, they were surprised and bewildered to see a big overstuffed chair and not the facilities they expected. If they had told Oscar what they needed, he would have directed them to the outhouse!

Later, it became a pool hall and beer parlor, home of regular buck euchre card games, eight ball, rotation and snooker. It deteriorated into a pretty skuzzy place that was referred to by almost everyone as the "Snake Pit". It burned down in 1965 and was never rebuilt.

Next was a small barbershop. It was torn down when I was still very young, but I remember getting my first haircuts in that little barbershop. The barber who came after that set up shop in what had been Bergo's Cafe across the street. Next door was Margaret's Beauty Shop, a building with metal siding built by Margaret's husband, Lubby Roberts. They lived upstairs with their family.

And next to the beauty shop was the Fairway Grocery store. This building is featured on the cover of the Faribault County Area Telephone Directory for 1999-2000 with a photograph from about 1912 when it housed the Nelson-Gunderson Hotel and Restaurant and the Underdahl Millinery Shop. It later became a general store owned and operated first by the Maland Brothers, John and Joseph, then by P. J. Erdal, then by his daughter, Inez and her husband, "Ike" Isakson. Ike and Inez lived upstairs with their family and P. J. (Pete) had a room there.

The old Post Office, Gullord's Hardware and P J Erdal's store

Ike operated a general store in that double frame building with groceries on one side and dry goods on the other. You could buy everything you needed in that store – fresh fruits and vegetables, canned goods, dairy products, breakfast cereals, bakery goods, shoes and socks, overalls, ready made clothes, fabrics, thread, buttons and everything else needed to make your own clothes and much more. I remember a display of reading glasses that you could try on to find a pair to help you see better. Later Ike built an addition to the back of the store behind the dry goods and put in a meat counter and a frozen food locker plant.

Willmert's Café, State Bank, Post Office, Ike's Fairway Foods

Ike was a good merchant. He was very progressive and rebuilt his display shelves often, rearranging the merchandise whenever he saw a better or fresher way to display goods. I remember when he changed from the old style store to self-service. Before that, you would give your order to Ike, or whoever was at the counter, and they would get it for you from shelves behind the counter. He bought the farmers' eggs—often in exchange for groceries. My brother, Jim, and I worked for him candling the eggs. One of Ike's regular customers had the worst eggs I ever saw. He kept them too long before bringing them in and to make it even worse, the eggs and paper separators were always wet and smelly. We usually had to throw out most of his eggs, but Ike had given us standing orders that this customer would always get 100% Grade A ratings so that Ike could give him the highest possible price. Ike's reasoning was that the customer had a big family and was very poor and needed the money. It was a good lesson in the true meaning of charity and being our brother's keeper.

Inez Isakson at the counter in the dry goods department

One day I was cleaning a shelf in the back room of Ike's store. There in a dark corner, unseen and untouched for many years, was a boxed bottle of patent medicine. The box had a picture of a sweet–looking little girl with blond curls. Around the picture, was the slogan, "I know it's pure, because my Daddy makes it". The last owner of that store was Art Ackerman. He closed the business in June 1986.

The next building, Our Own Hardware, was owned by Ted Gullord who was also my Dad's boss by virtue of his ownership of most of the shares in the bank. Ted wanted to teach me how to be a sheet metal worker. I remember cutting a large sheet of tin and using a device that could shape it to be used as a heating duct. I lost interest in that idea very quickly but I didn't have the nerve to tell Ted. As soon as he went "out front" to wait on a customer, I slipped out the back door and kissed that career goodbye!

Some years later, Earl Sather bought the hardware store and after a few years moved it to larger quarters in the Jensvold building. Earl moved to Frost from Minneapolis. His brother was married to my cousin so I was sort of related to him. He loved to play along with the joke when someone sent a young kid to the hardware store to get a "left-handed monkey wrench" or a "sky-hook". Once when the axle of my bicycle broke, I took the wheel assembly apart and brought the two broken halves of the axle to the hardware store and asked Charlie Besendorf, Earl's helper, for "an axle just like this one". Charlie said he could help me but that it would take awhile. When I asked why, he said it would take a lot of work to twist a new one and break it in half, "just like this one".

Earl was an interesting man and made quite an impression on me. He was the scoutmaster and was "cut from different cloth" than most of the other adults I knew. When we had trouble starting a campfire in the true boy scout manner by rubbing sticks, he produced a small flask of kerosene, splashed a little on the firewood and gave us a match. It was a much faster method! Earl set up an informal bar in the back room of the hardware store every December and gave free drinks to his customers (at least to those who wanted one). This was not long after prohibition had been repealed and there were lots of people, including my parents, who did not approve of liquor. (My Dad kept a pint bottle hidden in the basement "for medicinal purposes", but I never saw him take a drink from it.) Earl was about 6 feet 6 inches tall and had been a Golden Gloves boxer in his youth. One of his customers was an unwashed, heavy-set farmer who wore the same clothes for months at a time, never shaved and was surly and scared all us kids just seeing him walk by. Once Earl was fixing the man's sink and apparently not doing it fast enough when the man got angry and kicked him. Earl got up from under the sink and without a word, delivered his best punch and knocked the man out cold. As Earl walked out he told the astonished wife "when he wakes up, tell him to find someone else to fix your sink!"

Next came the old post office. The people in town either had a mailbox at the post office or asked for their mail at the window. People in the country had delivery service. There was an outhouse behind the post office. One Halloween when we thought nobody used that outhouse any longer, we weren't satisfied with just tipping it over—a fate destined for most owners of outhouses. We tipped it back up and over again and again until the roof fell off and then we tipped it up and over again and again until it collapsed and folded more or less flat.

Beside the post office was a vacant lot where band concerts and ice cream socials were held in the summer. The vacant lot was also a great spot for games like "kick-the-can", "pump, pump, pull away", "enny eye over" and "olly olly oxen free". In the winter, we made a large wheel in the snow with spokes and a hub by tramping pathways in the snow and played "fox and geese" on the wheel.

The corner building was the State Bank of Frost where my Dad was the banker. I remember when the old-fashioned teller cages were removed for a more modern and open look. A grandfather's clock stood at the end of the counter. My nephew, Jeff Kittlesen, now has that clock in his home.

Clifford Kittlesen at Cashier's desk, Click at left

When I was about two years old, a lone gunman robbed the bank. I was too young to remember the robbery but I do remember hearing about it. Growing up as a banker's son made it hard for me to see the "glamour" that Hollywood liked to portray in the lives of bank robbers. My sister Naomi remembers one day when Dad went into work very early and found a window open with water on the floor from the intruder's shoes. Apparently a noise or something scared the thief into leaving before Dad got there, but that was the last time Dad was motivated to go to the bank that early in the morning!

State Bank of Frost. The morning after the 1934 robbery

Dad at his desk in 1939. Note the telephone on his wall.

Clifford Kittleson was named cashier of the State Bank of Frost in 1930. He makes many decisions for the bank and is acclaimed as an able adviser to patrons of the institution on financial matters. The past several months he and his staff have been busy supervising the redecorating of the interior of the bank for the fortieth anniversary.

In January 1957, the ownership of the bank changed. My brother Click became the new president and my sister Dorothy was elected assistant cashier and board member.

Retiring and new directors of the State Bank of Frost are shown during the meeting last Wednesday in which Clifford Kittlesen, Jr., third from left, front, was named president and managing officer of the 68-year-old banking firm. Retiring board members are T. H. Gullord; Alfred J. Brandsoy, who will continue work in the bank for a short while; John J. Nelson and Iver B. Satre.

In front row, left to right, are Satre; Mrs. Dorothy Nesheim, new board member and assistant cashier; President Kittlesen; and Palmer N. Eckhardt, promoted from assistant cashier to cashier. Back row, Nelson, Gullord, Brandsoy and Clifford Kittlesen, Sr., a remaining board member who has been bank president.

A major addition was built on the north side of the bank in 1967 and the interior was completely remodeled.

Front view of addition   Rear view shows new Maland's

Across the street, the third block began with what was originally the Franklin Drug Store and Hotel, a general store with departments for groceries, hardware, men's and women's clothing, shoes and hats. My first memory of that

51

building was delivering newspapers to the apartments upstairs. At that time it was Charlie Schroeder's Tavern. The tavern closed during World War II and the building was converted later into the REC (Rural Electric Cooperative) office and later still into Ronnie Wilmert's Café. I remember one of Ronnie's waitresses telling me that she was never going to get married. "I'm going to be an old maid and teach all my kids to be the same," she'd say! Ronnie's Cafe was a good place to hang out. This building is now the Frost Post Office and is one of the few buildings left on Main Street.

The next building had been a restaurant, pool hall and offices for the Frost Record newspaper before it became Leonard's Cafe, Jonie's Cafe, Burton and Devere's Plumbing and Heating, Tim's Cafe and finally a community cafe. The cafe was another hangout for us kids when we weren't playing pool at the Snake Pit. It was the drop–off point for my daily supply of the Minneapolis Star and Sunday Tribune newspapers. My delivery route started there and I can still remember walking north along Main Street, then west towards the school, back east along the north edge of town and then south towards home to finish. The café was also the only place in town where you could buy magazines and comic books. I remember seeing a magazine in the rack with an article about life in small town America. That caught my eye and I started reading. When I got to a reference to one "small town of 70,000 population" I quit reading that article. I remember wondering if 70,000 was small, what were we with a population of 300?

Leonard chewed tobacco as many men did in those days and had spittoons in the café, like many stores did. He often sat on a stool behind the counter waiting for more business. One day I was sitting at the counter, probably eating or drinking something, when he let fly with a wad of tobacco across the counter to the spittoon on the other side! I thought that was pretty disgusting and he probably wouldn't have done it if grownups were around. A few days later his daughter, Leona, was working behind the counter and she asked me if we had spittoons in our house. I said: "Of course not" and she replied, "we have them all over our house!" I was sure that chewing tobacco would vanish when the old pioneers died off and have been surprised and disappointed to see such a lousy habit make a comeback, especially among young people.

Jonie and his wife Gladys ran a friendly place. Gladys was a friend to all the kids in town. She died very suddenly and unexpectedly at a very young age, 35 or 36, I think. That was a very sad time for her family and everyone in town.

After Gladys died, Burton Njoes and DeVere Brekke bought the building and started a plumbing and heating business. They also sold the first television sets in town. They always had a TV set on as a demo, a big attraction at the time. I remember watching the Minneapolis Lakers play basketball at their store. TV reception was not very good in those days and there were times when it looked like the Lakers were playing in a snowstorm! Arlene Njoes recalls providing homemade popcorn to the kids as they gathered to watch television at the store.

Tim Njoes, Burton's brother, made the building a café again. That place always was a popular place for kids and adults to "hang-out". After the community café closed, the building deteriorated and ended its existence when it was intentionally burned to give the volunteer firemen a live practice training session. A sad end for a great place.

Next door was Martin Kallestad's Meat Market. Martin always had a smile for the kids and would give us a free, good-tasting wiener cold from the meat counter. He had a smokehouse in back and made his own sausages and smoked his own hams. After he merged his business with Ike, his building became another cafe, run by Shorty Forthun. Shorty and his wife converted the smokehouse into their living quarters. They kept their extra change in a cloth bag and stored it in the ice cream freezer until needed to replenish the cash register. If you got your change direct from the freezer, as I often did, Shorty always called it "cold cash". It was! Shorty's Café became a hotbed for political discussion. Ernest Anderson's career as a state senator began in those discussions.

The popcorn stand stood between the meat market and the Red and White grocery store. The store was built in 1902 by Rasmus Brekke, or as we always knew him, "R. M." He and I. A. Hanson operated a general store with groceries and dry goods. A. A. Erdahl bought out I. A. Hanson's interest the next year. (We had lots of people who were known by their initials in those days.) Later owners were a Mr. Fielding and Carl Engeseth. Juhl Wilmert bought the store the year after I was born and ran a grocery store there for the next ten years or so until he sold it to Presley Williamson. Presley moved to Frost from Baudette, on the Canadian border, with his family. His son Walter was my age and my ticket to a career in the popcorn stand. The popcorn stand was the focal point in town on free show nights and working there brought some social status. I liked that job a lot.

Walter and I also sprouted a huge bin of potatoes in the store basement. We were promised a dollar each for removing all the sprouts and that sounded good at the time. I think we were at the task of removing sprouts and throwing out rotten potatoes for months—well at least for a week or more! Anyway, it seemed endless and should have been worth a lot more than a dollar each but that was the bargain and that's what we got. I didn't like that job at all!

The Red & White grocery was owned next by Lester Stoll. I delivered groceries for Les Stoll. He had a sporty new Nash coupe that was fun to drive but then I had just gotten my driver's license so I guess it was fun to drive anything! Next it became the Glen-Ray Grocery owned by Glen

Nesheim and Ray Hanson and owned by Ray alone when Glen moved on to a career with Super Valu grocery distributors.

I had many memorable experiences working for Ray Hanson. He had a great sense of humor and lots of common sense. A young man, new to Frost, parked his new car in front of the store one day. I said something about how successful he was to have such a fancy new car at such a young age. Ray replied, "Maybe he is, but don't be fooled by a new car. Any damn fool can borrow money". I think he understood more about consumer credit then than many people do now! Lots of people charged their groceries in those days and paid their bill once a week or once a month. One day while I was working at the front counter, Lloyd Larson came in and paid his charges. Ray gave him a carton of cigarettes as a thank you, something he did regularly. Gene Clark was buying his groceries for cash and observed the bonus. He asked Ray, "Why do you give him free cigarettes for using your money and give me nothing for paying cash?" It was a good question. I don't recall if Ray changed his practice but I do remember him talking with me about the unfairness of an accepted practice and wondering how he could change it. Wages and prices were much, much lower in those days, but I remember Ray tallying up the day's sales and being very happy with a $200 gross in sales for the day!

While I was working for Ray, he came down with scarlet fever. It was the third time he had had it and it left him with a severely damaged heart. He was in bed in their apartment for months. Dean Midthun had been taking care of the meat counter for Ray. When Dean left for better things, I took over the duties of a "meat man". It was a lot better than candling eggs! I did OK as meat man for the most part and enjoyed dealing with my customers, ordering the sides of beef and pork and the sausages, etc as they were needed. I learned how to take advantage of special prices, order only the items that would sell in our town and how to make "the best hamburger in town". Hamburger was a lead item for the store. One day I discovered, to my dismay, a pan of chuck meat that I had prepared for grinding more than a few days earlier. It didn't look good and it didn't smell fresh. I knew I was in trouble but I took some of it upstairs to show Ray and ask what to do with it. "Throw it out", was Ray's immediate reaction. "Wouldn't it be OK to mix it in with some fresh meat?" I asked. Ray replied, "We just couldn't let even one person to get sick from it and besides, that would be the end of the business". He wasn't mad at me; in fact, he thanked me for coming to him with the problem.

Gwendolyn Quam worked at Ray's grocery while I was there. We used to talk a lot when we weren't busy with customers. I remember when she asked me what my mailing address would be in the fall when I went off to college. I asked her who wanted to know, thinking it might be a girl for whom I had a secret crush. "Oh, someone" she replied. Gwen was the most popular girl in town and I couldn't imagine she might want to write to me. A few months later, Gwen was killed in a motorcycle accident. It was a terrible tragedy for everyone in our little town. I never received any letters from a Frost girl while I was in college. Could Gwen have been the "someone"?

Joe Kallestad worked at the store and was in charge when Ray was sick. One day he was sitting on a high stool at the desk in the back of the store totally absorbed working on the charge accounts. Dean and I poked holes in both ends of an egg and blew all the egg yolk and white out. Then we put a little warm water in the egg, walked up behind Joe pretending to be interested in what he was doing. Without warning, we crushed the egg on the back of his head so that the warm water ran down his neck and back. It must have felt like egg white and yolk and he yelped and chased both of us around the store until he caught the slower of us, unfortunately me. He dragged me to the back of the store where the eggs were stored. Dean and I were laughing too hard to explain that it was only water. Joe probably wouldn't have listened if we had told him. He grabbed a real egg and smashed it on my head. Even with egg yolk and white in my hair and face and down my neck, I couldn't stop laughing. It was worth it to see his reaction to our joke!

Ray was a good friend and a good businessman. Unfortunately, he never really recovered from the effects of the scarlet fever. He had to sell the store because it was more than he would ever be able to handle again. He was able to work again as the business manager of the school but died a few years later, in his 30's, leaving Wanda and six children.

The corner building was built originally as an Opera House. Amund Brekke showed movies there and brought in vaudeville entertainment, lectures and concerts. The lectures included temperance meetings and religious meetings of an organization known as the Black Sox Cult. It later became the produce building where you could buy baby chickens to raise, or freshly killed and dressed chickens ready for cooking. A new co-op gas station and garage replaced it about the time World War II ended. Otis Honstad ran an auto repair business in the back of the station and helped me keep my '37 Ford running. He taught me how to do some of the repairs myself and was always generous in letting me use his tools and equipment.

The fourth and final block had no businesses, just two homes. The corner house was where the school superintendent, P. S. (Pearly) and Mary Hegdal lived with their children: Margaret, Paul and Kathy.

Cliff Shuster lived in the last house until we moved there when I was in about the seventh grade. Just south of us was platted to be Front Street, but the street was never built and it provided space for a huge garden for our family. Dad was an avid gardener; I was a reluctant weeder!

Living next door to the school superintendent presented a major challenge. The problem for me with my Dad and Pearly Hegdal being neighbors was my dubious ability for getting in trouble in school. My voice carried too well. (I think that sounds better than saying I have a big mouth!) As a result, whenever discipline broke down in the classroom, I was the one sent to the superintendent's office. (We didn't get sent to the principal's office because there wasn't one.) I was sure that Pearly would say something to my Dad about my conduct. He never did as far as I know. Our families became close friends; my sister Helen and Kathy are still good friends all these years later.

An early view of the railway depot in Frost

The Chicago and Northwestern Railway depot was located at the south end of Main Street. It was an especially busy place during sugar beet season. Sugar beets were a very big crop for the farmers around Frost. It was a labor-intensive crop requiring lots of hand work in those days. The beet farmers all hired Mexican migrant workers who lived in makeshift shacks on each farm during the growing and harvesting season. Frost was the sugar beet capital of the world!

During harvest season, dozens of trucks came to town and lined up down the street behind our house waiting their turns to have the load weighed and dumped into a bin with a conveyor belt that lifted the beets up and into the railroad cars. The truck drivers had to sit in their trucks waiting for their turn and were always interested in getting cigarettes or candy treats while they were waiting. It was a great opportunity for me. I would take their orders and their money and go to the store for them. They always gave me a generous tip for the service. It was good for them and for me. The crop came in faster than the railroad could transport the beets to the sugar refinery in Mason City, Iowa. The solution to that problem was simply to stack the beets in enormous piles along the railroad tracks and then load them into trains later. I think they were loaded into open cars like the ones used to haul coal (maybe the same cars used for coal).

Unloading sugar beets. Huge piles like this lined the tracks.

The road to the beet dump served as our driveway also and since there was no truck traffic in the winter, the county snow plow truck ignored the street and I had to shovel a VERY long drive. I remember one snowstorm that left about 3 feet of snow. I was struggling with a heavy shovel and heavy snow when the snowplow headed towards the corner where it always turned to miss us and get the busier streets. Johnny Njoes operated the county plow. He saw me just getting started, waved at me to get out of the way and plowed all the snow away, right up to our garage doors! I always had liked Johnny and that day he was my best grown-up friend!

On the other side of the tracks were the Farmer's Co-op Elevator and the coal sheds and the oil and gasoline storage tanks. The grain elevator caught fire one night in about 1944 or 1945. It was very close to our house and a spectacular sight. Fire departments from the surrounding towns were called in to help contain the fire and keep it from spreading by pouring water from their hoses onto the coal sheds and gasoline storage tanks. The thought of those gasoline tanks exploding was uppermost on everyone's mind until the fire had pretty much consumed the elevator and was reduced to a smoldering mess that couldn't do any more damage.

The Frost fire truck performed well but the "hose" truck wouldn't start and had to be pushed to the fire by a group of men. It seemed like everyone in town ended up on our lawn to watch the fire and many of them used our bathroom during the long evening. As the fire intensified, dozens, maybe hundreds of rats fled from the doomed structure. Our poor Mother was torn between being a good sport and letting everyone continue to use our one bathroom, or finally saying "no more" because she was terrified that rats would come into our house with the door opening and closing so many times.

Late in the evening, about midnight as I recall, a freight train arrived on its regular run. It stopped while the firemen and the engineer debated whether it was safe for the train to continue. It had to pass within a few feet of the burning elevator. The fire was still burning openly, but only at the top. After a long discussion, the engineer finally decided to chance it. The firemen kept pouring water from their hoses on the train as the engineer pulled the train slowly and safely past the fire.

Men from the fire departments were there all night and for several days after as the fire slowed but continued until the elevator was gone. The grain pits went deep into the ground and continued to burn for weeks, maybe months. The cleanup was a long one and we kids liked to help by squirting the hoses into the smoldering mess. Many of the kids in town had trap lines and sold the pelts from the animals they trapped. Those kids, including my brother Jim, were called into action to rid the town of the rats that had escaped from the fire. The town businessmen offered a 25 cents bounty for every rat tail turned in. The scheme was a great success. The kids made lots of money and the rat problem was quickly eliminated! German soldiers, prisoners of war from a camp near Fairmont, were brought in to help with the cleanup. They were all "trustees" and no one worried about them being enemy soldiers. We kids talked with them and found them to be interesting and "good" people.

Ollie Savick, the depot and the new elevator complex.

On the east side of Main Street (moving back north) were three homes in the first block, Alfred Graues, Ruby Brekke's, and Nelmer Sabins. Nelmer had a speech impediment that resulted in a sound "huh" that prefaced every sentence and many words within his sentences. He was a good-natured guy with a good sense of humor. At the time, eyeglasses were beginning to be a fashion item. Nelmer ran into Ollie Savick and his grandson,

Buddy, one day. Buddy had just started wearing glasses. Nelmer asked, "Is he wearing them for huh-looks or for huh-necessity?" Ollie replied, "Oh, he needs them all right". Nelmer came back with, "Well, I was going to say if he was wearing them for huh-looks, he's putting in a huh-hell of a lot of huh- time for huh-nothing!" Everyone called him Huh-Nelmer.

The first corner building on the next block is a fuzzy memory for me. It was a very old wooden frame building with outside stairs to the second floor. The grounds around the building were littered with all kinds of farm machinery, new and used, some of it ready for the junk yard. Jensvold's Implements bought the site and replaced the old building with a new large modern brick building. They sold farm machinery, tractors, cultivators, plows and other farm implements and major household appliances.

The next business was Ted Nesheim's garage. Ted started with a blacksmith shop and also fixed farm equipment. When the first cars arrived in Frost, Ted taught himself how to fix them. It was common knowledge that "if Ted couldn't fix it, it couldn't be fixed". Ted was also a self-taught violinist and played frequently for church and school programs. He was a man of many talents and the father of my brother-in-law, Kenny.

Just north of Ted's garage was a vacant lot where the circus set up its tents and stakes for elephants. I can't remember what year the circus came to Frost, or whether it came more than once. Later, when a well was dug for a city water supply, a new brick building was built there to house the water tank (no water tower for Frost). The new building also housed the fire trucks and served as the town hall.

The volunteer firemen had an annual corn roast at the school to raise funds for the fire department. Freshly picked sweet corn, still in its husks, would be stuffed into gunnysacks and then soaked with water from their fire hoses. Fire pits were dug and hot fires were built in them. When the coals were hot enough they would throw the gunnysacks full of corn on top of the glowing coals. The result was smoked delicious sweet corn everyone enjoyed to their hearts' content! I'm sure we had lots of other good food to go with it but all I can remember is the taste of that wonderful smoked corn. One year, when I had stuffed myself with smoked corn, I stopped at Folken's cafe on my way home and had a cherry malted milk. It was the proverbial straw that broke the camel's back. I got sick from my foolish excess and the combined tastes of smoked corn and cherry malt stayed with me for years afterward. Whenever I drank a cherry malted milk, I could actually taste a heavy smoked flavor. Finally, after about 20 years of not being able to enjoy the cherry flavor by itself, I gave up and decided I would never be able to have another cherry malted milk. It took about another 20 years of "abstinence" before I felt it just might be possible, so I tried again and to my delight, was able to enjoy a cherry malt for its own great flavor.

 Next door was Alfred Brandsoy's harness shop. I remember the rich smell of the leather and oil. Alfred had a large tank full of oil and a mesh basket that could be lowered into the tank to soak leather harnesses, saddles, etc. He had huge sewing machines that could stitch and repair all sorts of leather products. When horses were no longer used for farming, the harness shop closed. Alfred went to work in the bank and his building later became Henderson's Cafe. Mr. Henderson was well known for the most generous home-packed ice cream. He packed the cartons so tight it seemed like you got a lot more for your money. It was a little messy so you were likely to get his thumbprints on the top flaps as a "bonus".

 The next building, on the corner of the block, was built with diamond-faced concrete blocks and had a curved roof. It served many purposes; first as a repair shop, gas station and a new car show room for Brush and Allen automobiles, then as a warehouse and storage garage for the Rural Electric Cooperative's trucks, then as a warehouse for onions, and sometimes as just a large open enclosed space where we could ride our bicycles and play games. We rode our bikes around the abandoned grease pit (wedged into a tight corner) and pretended we were taking off in our airplanes to fight German or Japanese planes doing our part to win World War II. I missed the corner one fateful day and fell to the bottom of the grease pit with my bicycle on top of me and my front teeth broken in half.

Our Frost dentist, Doc Johnson, was off fighting the real war and so I ended up in the care of an elderly dentist in Blue Earth. Maybe he would have been retired by then if the war hadn't taken all the young dentists and maybe he just wasn't up to date on the latest methods, but he said the broken teeth were beyond repair and pulled them out. I think I was about eleven years old. I went through high school and early dating with a series of partial plates. Because I was in my growing years, I outgrew each plate almost as soon as I got it so they never fit quite right. Food particles were always getting between the plate and the roof of my mouth. It drove me nuts, was embarrassing and grossed out everyone who caught me with my teeth out or, worse yet, half out while I was trying to get rid of the offending particles. If you have ever had a stone in your shoe, you have some idea what it was like to have a bit of peanut or other hard food under a partial plate! Maybe this explains why I never had a date until I was in college and had learned to be more discreet about cleaning my teeth! When I was 24 years old, I was finally able to get a bridge to replace my partial plate. It was right after my military service and Doc Johnson found a cavity in one of the teeth next to the open space. He applied to the Veteran's Administration for me and got their authorization to put a gold cap on that tooth, in effect paying for about half the cost of the new bridge.

The creamery stood in the block behind that corner garage building. Farming was diversified then and most farmers had cows that produced more than enough milk for their own needs. The surplus milk was trucked into town in the milk cans you now see in antique stores. The operator of the creamery was known as "the buttermaker." Cliff Schuster, then Harvey Menk and then Emery Johnson, made butter to serve the community's needs and more. So Frost Creamery butter was one of our exports. I wish I knew how far it traveled and to what communities.

Across the street on the corner was Maland's Supply. Leo Maland operated an auto repair service, a gasoline filling station and a store that sold radios and phonographs, among many other things for homes and autos. In the early days, Leo's service used hand–operated pumps that filled a glass container at the top to the requested number of gallons. Then a valve was opened, gravity took over and the gas flowed through a hose down to the car's tank. I remember when the first modern electric gas pump was installed. The photo below shows Maland's Supply with one new pump and two of the old ones. Except for the transition as they replaced the old pumps, it looked like this during all of my growing up years.

Maland's Supply with Joseph J. Maland at the pumps

I bought a table model radio phonograph from Leo that included a 78 rpm record changer. It was exciting to be able to stack 12 records at a time and have almost half an hour of uninterrupted music! I was able to buy it because it was on sale at half price since this was just about the time that 33 1/3 and 45 rpm records began to make 78s obsolete. But I didn't care. My new phonograph was great after having grown up with my parent's Victrola and later my brother Jim's record player that was powered by electricity instead of a hand crank wind-up device but that only played one record at a time. In fact, Jim only had one record to play on it for months. It was a happy day when he finally was able to start buying more records and we were able to have a little musical variety!

Archie (Hawkey) Carlson worked for Leo. He was always good for a laugh. Once he was washing his own car during a slow time at the station. He washed one side, half of the trunk and half of the hood, put the hose away and started walking across the street towards the bank. Someone hollered, "Hey, Hawkey, aren't you going to finish the job?" He replied, "Not until I ask Clifford if he wants to have his half washed!"

A small building behind Maland's served as the first Rural Electric Cooperative office and also as a beauty shop and later as the town hall for a while.

Just north of Maland's Supply was an empty lot where we had free shows every Saturday night. The Frost businessmen's association built a large movie screen and bleachers, provided the projector and rented the movies. They showed the movies free to everyone. The pay theaters in Bricelyn and Blue Earth were too expensive (12 cents for kids) and too far away for us to see many movies. Oh, and if you did get to see a good movie, you only saw it once—no reruns, no video rentals—no VCR's—no way to ever own a movie in those days! At some point, Wednesday night became free show night instead of or maybe in addition to Saturday night and in the wintertime, the free movies were shown in the school building.

The older viewers sat in the bleachers and the kids sat on blankets on the ground. We all watched great comedians like Laurel and Hardy, Abbot and Costello, the Little Rascals and Buster Keaton; we saw cowboys like Gene Autry, Roy Rogers and Tom Mix. We also watched B-movies (do you remember that term?) and anything else that could be rented for a reasonable price. There was a wooden fence and entry area behind the bleachers to block the headlights of the cars parking and leaving. I've been told that there was a time when the bleachers were segregated with the migrant workers on one side and the town residents and farmers on the other. Maybe so, but I only remember that kids sat on the ground and grown ups sat on the bleachers.

The popcorn stand was down in the next block next to the Red and White Grocery so there were always people walking in the street competing with the cars. I guess we never heard about crossing the street at a corner. One Saturday night I was in a hurry to watch the movie and not paying attention as I crossed the street and a car ran over my foot. The driver never noticed and I didn't give it much thought either. The car was a Model T Ford and it was so light that I hardly felt anything. I just remember thinking "that's strange, I've been run over and it doesn't even hurt!"

That reminds me of a friend who always ran across the street and then stopped and turned around to look for cars. I asked him why he didn't look first. He said his mother told him to "look both ways *when* you cross the street. I tried to convince him she meant to look *before* crossing, but he insisted that *when* meant *after*. I couldn't convince him that it didn't do much good to look after getting hit by a car.

Next to the free show lot was Dr. Hanson's first office where I had my tonsils removed when I was six years old.

There was an addition on the north side of Doc's building that housed Bergo's Cafe and later, Ed Bartel's barber shop. When Doc moved his office, Ed and Mildred moved in and lived in what had been Doc's offices. Ted Gullord's place was next door. He used it as an office and warehouse for his hardware store. Doc Johnson built a dental clinic on the adjacent lot. It later became the village office (town hall). Doc Hanson used the house on the corner lot as his second office. When Doc Johnson arrived in Frost, he rented a room from Doc Hanson in that building to use as his first dental office. The Emerald Lutheran Church occupied the corner lot across the street.

Ollie Savick, the railway depot agent and telegraph operator lived in the house next to the church. His daughter married Earl Davidson and had a son, Earl, Jr. They were living somewhere out west when her husband drowned. She was unable to take care of her son and work to support herself so she brought her son, known as Buddy, home to Frost where her parents could care for him. The kids in town had not known Buddy's father and it was natural for everyone to call him Buddy Savick. When he started school, the teacher (new that year) called the roll. When she called for Earl Davidson, Jr., all the kids turned around to see who the new kid was and were amazed to see "Buddy Savick" answer "here". His grandfather, Ollie, was everyone's friend and a second Dad to all the kids.

Doc Hanson and his wife, Gert, built their first house next to Ollie. One Halloween someone tipped over a pile of logs to block Doc's garage door. I remember seeing the so-called prank with some friends as we were making our rounds and doing our own mischief. Trick or Treat was unknown to us. We only knew about tricks but this one struck us as a stupid and terrible thing to do. "What if someone gets sick and Doc needs to use his car to make a house call?" We went to work and moved the heavy logs out of the way so he could get his car out if he needed to. It may have been our only good deed on a Halloween night. Next to Hansons, Martin Kallestad lived in the corner house with his family.

At the north end of Main Street, there was a dairy farm operated by Maynard Helseth. He provided home delivery of the pasteurized milk from his cows. It was a complete farm where the cows lived and grazed and gave their milk. Maynard separated the cream, pasteurized and bottled the milk and delivered it to everyone's back porch. He drove a Model T with a lot of clearance underneath and could easily drive through any amount of snow in the predawn hours before the snowplow cleared the streets and alleys. The glass milk bottles sat on the porch long enough on a cold day for the milk to begin to freeze, pushing the cardboard milk cap several inches higher than the top of the bottle. I didn't see milk caps for many years until they resurfaced a few years ago as "pogs" for kids to buy and collect. Milk wasn't homogenized in those days so we could shake it for "regular milk" or pour off the cream first for coffee and/or whipped cream and use the rest as skim or low-fat milk, although I don't remember anyone ever calling it that.

Church

The Emerald Lutheran Church was always located on Main Street during my years in Frost but it began in 1869 with meetings in the homes of pioneer farmers, about 30 years before Frost existed. According to one story, when someone suggested that it was time to start having services in English, the farmer who was hosting that meeting said, "Well, if you can't have services in Norwegian, you can move the church off my land"! So a new church was built in 1888 next to the cemetery in Emerald Township just about a mile north and west of town.

In 1915, some of the members wanted to move the Emerald church to town, but others were opposed to the move. In the middle of the night, the supporters of the move put logs under the building and with a team of horses, moved the church into town. The next morning when the town awoke, the move was complete and the debate was over. This story may be in question, because Larry Anderson recalls his father describe watching the building being moved in broad daylight and a building that size would have required some time to move. Another story referred to it as the "stolen church". Clearly there was less than unanimous support for change!

The Emerald Lutheran Church on Main Street in Frost

The Frost Lutheran Church was built in 1902 with continuing financial support by the Dell Lutheran Church congregation. Dell was a small settlement in the valley along the banks of the Blue Earth River. A parsonage (for the pastor serving both congregations) was built next door to the Dell church and remained there all through my growing-up years. When the only pastor I'd ever known retired about 1950, it was difficult to call a new young pastor to live in the country. As my Dad said, "When the child has outgrown the parent, it's time for the child to be on his own". A new parsonage was built in Frost in the late 1950's.

The Frost Lutheran Church as it looked for about 50 years

The recorded minutes of both congregations were originally written in Norwegian and it wasn't until 1924 that the Emerald minutes were first written in English. That same year, the minutes include the following: "It was moved, seconded and carried that we should stop with all trouble which has been prevalent". The next motion states: "It was moved and carried that we have one half English and one half Norwegian services". The minutes for the Frost congregation were not written in English until 1934. Those first minutes in English included the following: "Rev. H. O. Mosby gave a brief, but interesting report of the work carried on in the different branches of the church during the year". The next year, a motion called for the pastor to "conduct three regular Sunday morning services in the American language and one in the Norwegian language each month".

The two churches became congregations of the same Lutheran Synod as the result of a merger in 1917. However, they went their separate ways for another 30 years before they became one congregation. I always thought they merged and perhaps most of the town thought so too. Years later, I heard a story that both congregations were dissolved and the next day a new congregation, United Lutheran Church of Frost, was formed since that was easier than getting agreement to a merger. There is considerable doubt about this story also, as the final minutes of both churches show unanimous votes to unite.

The building that had housed the Emerald church was moved and joined to the Frost church building as part of a remodeling and expansion project. Part of the Emerald building became the choir loft and since we didn't have a choir, it was possible for everyone to sit in "their church" if they wanted.

We all took part in the annual Christmas program at the church. Each of the kids had a piece to memorize and we would stand up in the chancel, one class at a time, and recite what we had memorized. The church janitor, Ole Hjelle, would sit in the back row during rehearsals so Mrs. Alfred Brandsoy, the Sunday school superintendent, reminded everyone to speak up, "so Ole can hear you".

One year during the big event, with the church packed with proud parents and friends and relatives, the first or second graders each gave their piece and when it was his turn, Michael Johnson, son of Obbie and Marion Johnson, boomed out *"can you hear me, Ole?"* It was one of the few times in those staid and proper days that I heard the church ring out with laughter. After the program was over, there was a bag of peanuts with some hard candy and a big juicy red apple for each of the children.

To be confirmed in the Lutheran Church involved a two-year learning process called "reading for the minister". We memorized Bible verses and studied Luther's Small and Large Catechisms. After two years of study, we had "Catechization", a program where the confirmands stood in front of the congregation and answered all of the "what does this mean" questions from the small catechism.

Jim Anderson and I were the only two kids in our confirmation class at church, so we knew that we would each have to answer half of the questions. What we didn't know was which half we each would be asked. So we dutifully learned them all and somehow survived the experience and were confirmed the next Sunday and, like all the others before us, took our first communion.

Jim Anderson,
Pastor Mosby,
Neil Kittlesen.

H. O. Mosby was our pastor all the years I was growing up. When he retired, the congregation gave him a new Chrysler, a deluxe model with plaid upholstery as I remember. I thought it was very generous of the congregation and it was. I learned much later how poorly pastors were paid in those depression and war years. The Frost church records show that Pastor Mosby "was kind enough to decrease his salary during the depression". The Mosby family lived in a parsonage in the country, at Dell, with a large vegetable garden. It was a necessity. People occasionally brought them chickens, eggs and other food items and once a year, at Christmas time, there was a special offering for the pastor. All the members of the congregation would march up to the front and around behind the altar and leave their contribution on the altar. In 1942, the records show that Pastor Mosby was given a cost of living increase of $100 in recognition of the fact that "living expenses have gone up considerably and that he voluntarily decreased his income during the depression years".

When the two Lutheran churches merged in 1947, the call committee recommended that the pastor's salary be set at $1,100 plus three holiday offerings. "After due consideration, Dr. Hanson moved that the congregation call Rev. Mosby at a salary of $1,250 and three holiday offerings. The motion was carried."

About that time, I remember seeing an annual report booklet for the church. In the back there was a list of every member with two columns of dollar amounts labeled "amount assessed" and "amount paid". I supposed those terms were used with good intentions and may have had some good effects on some of the members, but I have always thought that contributions to church and charitable organizations are "pledged and given", not "assessed and paid"!

Number Please

Frost had a local telephone company operated by a family from a house just half a block from Main Street. The switchboard was next to a window with an open view of people coming and going. When you made a call, you picked up the phone and the operator asked, "number please". There were no dials or buttons or area codes or ten digit local dialing or beeps in those days. I remember every family and business in Frost had only two digits for their telephone number.

Florence Loge was the chief telephone operator and her husband, Herman, was in charge of all the outside tasks of running the Frost Telephone Company. Their daughter, Mina, remembers it as a family business. They all took

Florence Loge on duty at Frost Telephone Central

turns at the switchboard as needed. When my mother wanted to call Dad she picked up the phone, gave the bank number: 22, and once, she recalled, Herman Loge responded; "he just walked over to the post office but he should be back at the bank in a few minutes". It *was* convenient; the families who ran the Frost Telephone Company during those years also provided an informal town receptionist service!

The telephone wasn't very private and Mom didn't like that part of the deal. We were lucky; we had a private line. Our number was 14. Many people, especially those who lived in the country, had two-three- or more party lines. Listening in on someone else's phone call was called rubber-necking and was very common. My brother John was on the line with Dorothy when she had a party line and she complained that she could hardly hear him. He replied "aw, it's just all the damn rubber-neckers!" and instantly they heard one click after another as they all hung up. Listening in was a great source for the latest gossip, but it was embarrassing in those days to get caught at it. The phone signals depended on batteries and every time another caller got on the line, the signal weakened. Nothing was very private in such a small town. Mother never gossiped, explaining she had never been able to keep track of who was related to whom— not easy for me either- we were about the only family who didn't seem to be related to almost every other family in town. The telephone stories could fill an entire book.

John Nesje, one of our famous Norwegian bachelors, walked past the grocery store where I was working one summer day. Ray Hanson, the grocer, poked his head out the door and said: "John, your wife called and said I should tell you to bring home a loaf of bread." John didn't look up or break stride as he retorted; "That's a damn lie, Ray, I ain't got no phone"!

Amund Brekke picked up his phone and when Pete Midthun, who was then the operator, asked, "number please", Amund said "56". Pete said "I'm sorry but I can't give you that number". Amund got more than a little agitated, and said something like, "you damn well better, Pete, I paid my phone bill". Pete replied, "OK, I'll plug you into your own hole and you can talk to yourself if you want to!"

My sister Naomi remembers: "I spent many hours there when Art and Lou Belau ran the telephone office. They once had such a tangle of wires plugged into the board that their only hope for survival was to pull them all out and start over again. Did Frost invent the conference call? When John called from Europe, Central would connect him to both the bank and the house. My favorite story is when Mother called Dad at noon and the operator informed her that he had just headed home, then asked if they should ring the store so they could tell him what to pick up as he went by."

Doc Hanson

When I was about four or five years old, I had a medical problem. My parents took me to see Doc. He examined me and told them that I would grow out of it. They felt he didn't take it seriously and took me to a doctor in Bricelyn whose diagnosis was that it was serious, that there was nothing he or anyone could do and that I would die. Dad's response was to tell the doctor that they weren't going to accept that and would take me to the Mayo Clinic for another opinion. The doctor replied that I was "a nice boy and worth saving". I think that made my Dad angry that this doctor would think there would be any child not worth saving. The doctors at the Mayo Clinic gave me a very thorough exam and I still remember the enemas they gave me! They concluded that Doc Hanson was right and that the problem was in fact one that I would grow out of and I did. My parents always trusted Doc Hanson after that experience.

We frequently played games in the vacant lot between the bank and the post office. One day while we were playing baseball I got hit in the eye with a baseball bat. I was the catcher and was crouched too close to the plate. Bill Isakson was the batter and he brought his bat back sharply to get ready for the next pitch. The bat struck me in the eye and I thought it drove my eyeball into the back of my head. I must have been about 10 or 11 years old and, fortunately, was not yet wearing glasses. Bill grabbed my hand and we went off to find Doc. He was just two doors away in the hardware store. He looked at my eye and told me that I would be all right. I asked if there would be any lasting effects and he replied, "Well, I'll tell you one thing, you'll get a hell of a shiner"! I did and that was the only ill effect besides a lot of pain.

Doc loved playing pool and when a guy came looking for him at the pool hall, and limped in, Doc asked what was wrong: "I think I broke my ankle" the guy said. "When did it happen", Doc asked. "Day before yesterday", was the reply. "Well, if you could wait until now to come see me, you can wait a little while longer while I finish this game", Doc said. "OK" was the reply and that seemed to satisfy everyone.

My niece, Karen Nesheim Parker, recalls getting a shot for her bronchitis in the middle of Main Street. He was driving off on an emergency when they flagged him down. "What do you need?" Doc asked through his open car window. When he learned that her bronchitis was flaring up again he told her to roll up her sleeve. He opened his bag, got the medicine she needed, opened his car door and gave her a shot of penicillin right there in the middle of Main Street and sped off to take care of the emergency. Karen also remembers another time when it was an emergency for her and in the middle of a blizzard. Doc asked Karen's mother, my sister Dorothy, what he could bring along for a treat. Karen loved Albert Lea Grape Pop. Doc got the pop and persuaded a farmer to take him to Rake on his tractor with the front loader because that was the only way that he could be sure of getting there in the storm. He gave her the medication she needed, the pop she wanted, and stayed at her bedside all night to be sure she would be all right.

Doc walked into the bank one day and asked, "who wants a flu shot?" Everyone wanted one so Doc opened his black bag, everyone rolled up their sleeves, and in no time at all they all had their shots! Another time, a woman brought her kids in to the clinic for booster shots. While Doc was taking care of one of the kids, the other ran out the back door and tried to hide from him. It was wasted effort, Doc ran out the door after the kid and caught him in a neighboring yard and gave him the shot while pinning him to the ground!

Ernest Anderson had problems with asthma. One winter night he was flat on his back and called for help. Doc drove out, gave him a shot and on his way out of the farmyard, his car got stuck. In a flash, he was back in the house and said "Get up, Ernie, I need a push".

When my Dad was seventy years old he had serious stomach pains after every meal. Doc examined him and was pretty sure it was cancer. He sent him to the hospital in Albert Lea for an x-ray. The report came back negative. Doc sent Dad back for another x-ray and again the report was negative. This time Doc got in his car immediately and drove the 30 miles to Albert Lea to see the x-ray for himself. "There it is, right there", he said as he examined the x-ray. Dad was operated on by Doc a few days later. After the operation, Doc showed Dad's stomach to my brother John and me. I still remember seeing Dad's entire stomach lying in a white enamel tray. Doc picked it up, sliced it open and showed us the huge cancerous growth that surely would have taken Dad's life very soon. Dad adjusted to life without a stomach quite well and had eight more good years, living to see his youngest daughter, Helen graduate from St Olaf College.

Kristin Bromeland Juliar posted this story on the Frost web site recently:"When I was 11, I dislocated my little finger the Sunday that the Twins were in the World Series. (in 1965) My mom drove me to Doc's house. He came out to the car, grumbling about being interrupted during the ball game, popped my finger back into place and told us to go "tape it up". You just don't get healthcare like that anymore!"

Doc had everyone's medical chart in his head and usually it included about three or more generations. His charges were always very low and he never mailed a bill to anyone. My son-in-law John Wentz recalls Doc making house calls for his family in Blue Earth. When his Dad asked Doc "How much do I owe you?" Doc replied "How about five dollars, does that sound about right?" He believed that people would pay him when (and if) they could. If they paid a little at a time or never at all, he accepted that as the way things were. It worked well for everyone, people got high quality care from a brilliant (he graduated number one in his class at the University of Minnesota Medical School) and dedicated physician and Doc was paid about 97 percent of the time.

Doc died in 1994. At the funeral, Larry Anderson delivered a tribute on behalf of all of us who knew and loved Doc. Larry gave me a copy of what he said to be included in this book:

"When the city of Frost recalls its first century, it is likely that no name will be more fondly remembered than that of Dr. Lewis Hanson. Perhaps no one will ever again touch so many lives in this community. Devoted to his family and his community, Doc truly became a legend in his own time. All the stories about Doc have one common thread. They are all stories about a country doctor, a brilliant man of compassion who tended to the needs of his neighbors nearly all the years of his life.

"Doc claimed to have delivered more than 3,000 babies –"Not bad" he would boast, "in a town of 300 people". We remember the school vaccination programs where Doc would give shots to the entire student body in a matter of minutes. Often before we could get our hands out of our pockets or our sleeves rolled up. We remember his instant emergency procedures during football games when Doc would rush in from the sidelines, pop joints back into place so fast that injured athletes didn't miss a play.

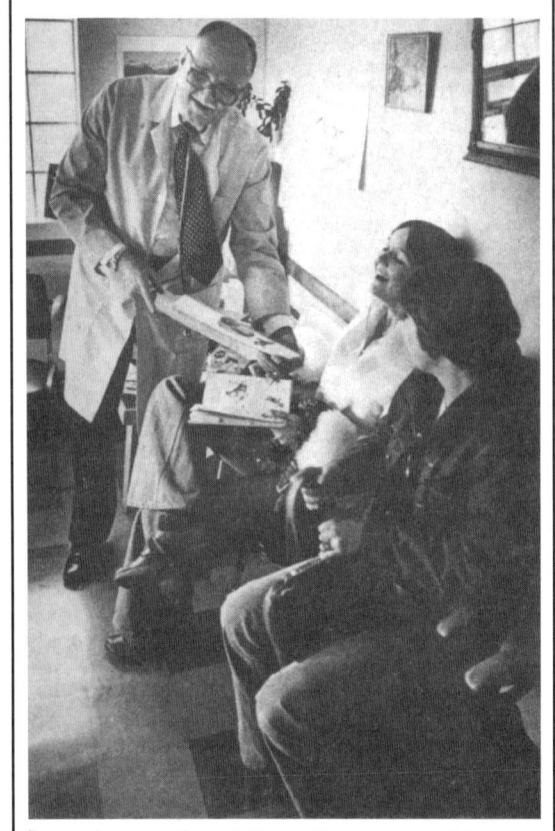

THE FREE PRESS
Saturday, Nov. 6, 1976—11

Doc makes sure those in the waiting room aren't bored.

"We remember Doc seeing more than 100 patients a day, some receiving treatment right in the waiting room to speed things along. Doc was always on duty, if you saw him in the post office and asked him to look at your throat, he would oblige. If you were sick at night you either went to his house or called him to make a house call. He always responded. He provided affordable access to rural medical service that politicians today will never understand or be able to duplicate. Doc was the end of an era.

"He was one of the first to see a need for an area nursing home and he became a primary promoter of the development of St Luke's Lutheran Home. Doc was concerned that the Frost area would need an ambulance after he retired. For years he had provided a "sort of" ambulance service by transporting patients in his car – often at speeds that scared people back to health. But he knew that the community must make plans to get along without him. He helped make things better by working with other leaders to develop a local volunteer ambulance service that continues to serve the area today. He served for years as chairman of the school board. He was a member and leader of his church. He donated land for what is now known as Hanson Park.

"Doc treated patients from Frost and Bricelyn and Rake and Kiester and most every other town within 50 miles. He was a wonderful physician because he knew us. He knew us not only as patients, he knew us as people, he knew us as neighbors, he knew us as family and friends."

School Days

When my family moved to Frost, there was just the old wooden frame schoolhouse that had been built in 1901. Its four classrooms housed eight elementary grades. Dorothy, Click, John and Jim attended the old school where I visited my brother Jim one day. I got to share his seat and desk and remember making a railroad track with clay on his desk. I'm not sure why such a small event sticks in my mind but we probably didn't have clay to play with at home. Anyway, it made one of those childhood impressions that last a lifetime. Dorothy, Click and John were bussed to Blue Earth for high school and Dorothy graduated from there.

The old wood frame school had four rooms for eight grades

Dorothy recalls that the school bus had a bench on each side and a third bench down the middle. She remembers that whenever the driver applied the brakes too hard, all the kids fell forward like dominoes! That is probably why someone got the bright idea to put in seats facing forward instead of benches.

The old and the new school buses

A new brick school was built in Frost to house twelve grades and opened in 1937. The old frame building was torn down to make room for a new playground. My brother Click was in the first class to graduate from the new high school in the spring of 1938 and his daughter Connie graduated in the second to last class before the school closed.

The new Frost school opened in 1937

The new playground. Would this swing be approved today?

I have many memories of my twelve years in that school. The three classrooms on the first floor held grades one, two and three in the first room, grades four, five and six in the second room, and grades seven and eight in the third room. Restrooms completed the first floor.

My first grade teacher was Esther Anderson and I have fond memories of her. She gave us a great start in our education. However, she was also very conscious of the importance of good hygiene and wanted to be sure that we had all washed our hands and faces every day before school. She made black and white hands from construction paper, glued them together and hung them in front of each row of desks. If everyone in the row had washed before school, that row would have a white hand displayed for the day. If even one of us had not, our row would get a black hand. I remember the day Sonny (Al) Underdahl responded that he had washed his face but not his hands! Esther tried to tell him that was impossible and that he had to wash his hands in order to wash his face. He insisted that he did wash his face without washing his hands and that was that. So our row got a black hand that day.

Esther Anderson

Everyone had clean hands today

Esther Anderson remembers, "Frost dedicated a new elementary and high school in September 1937. I became the teacher in grades 1, 2, 3 and 4. Frost was a loving community whose interest and activities centered around the school. Teachers were an integral part of this, and fond memories take me back to the hours we spent in their homes. There was a noteworthy Scandinavian influence. I taught there for four years. My ties to the community continued as I married Vernon Gronfor from Frost."

Grades 1, 2 and 3, 1939-1940

Grades 1,2 and 3

1940-1941

The four upstairs rooms included the library, which doubled as a class room for English and Biology, a classroom that doubled as our typing room and a study hall, another classroom (the only one that solely served that purpose) and the lab room where physics and chemistry were taught. For some unknown reason, we had algebra in the lab and biology in the library!

Who do you recognize?

A single stairway, on the southeast corner, took us to the upstairs classrooms, so a unique fire escape was built on the north side of the building. A large steel tube was fastened to the outside brick wall from the superintendent's office leading down to ground level. The superintendent's office was, in

85

effect, a hallway to the fire escape although doors that locked and unlocked only from the inside gave him some privacy. Whenever we had a fire drill, everyone in two of the upstairs classrooms marched single file through the superintendent's office and slid down the slide to "safety". The other two classes used the stairs, a more boring "escape". Of course, since the tube was open at ground level, we had a giant slide available anytime just by mastering the slippery climb up the tube. He never complained that I know of, but it must have been distracting for the superintendent to be trying to work on the other side of the doors at the top of the slide!

Frost High School under construction 1937 (note fire escape "tube")

A small gymnasium was attached on the west side of the building, a few steps down from the first floor classrooms. Three or four tiers of seats formed the bleachers on one side of the gym while a single row of benches lined each of the other three walls. During important basketball games, the crowds were so large that the benches were moved forward and people stood behind them in rows along the outer walls making the court even smaller—the 3 foot line became the out of bounds line.

Frost basketball team, 1937-1938
Front row: Elwood Johnson, Harlan Maland, Arthur Mosby, Gerhard Nepstad, Ignatius Hovland, Glen Nesheim, DeVere Brekke
Back row: Mr. Cottrell, Loren Midthun, Glen Thompson, Clifford Kittlesen, Thomas Sapa, Lester Egness, Allan Graue, Gerald Knutson, Mr. Syverson

Frost played 6 man football
Front row: Raymond Hanson, Harlan Maland, Arthur Mosby
Second row: Allan Graue, Lester Egeness, Glen Nesheim
Third row: Loren Midthun, Arden Egeness, Ralph Ficken, Allan Hanson, Donald Bromeland, Curtis Olson, Glen Thompson

Pep Club, 1937-1938
Front row: Audrey Engum, Miss Setterman, Jeanette Thompson
Second row: Serephine Egeness, Lucille Thompson, Aleida Davidson, Wanda Savick, Florence Nepstad, Ruth Mosby, Clarice Halvorson
Third row: Lailla Tenold, Della Savick, Shirley Voldahl, June Brekke, Iva Thompson, Canthaline Carlson, Orva Thompson
Fourth row: Iva Oppedahl, Eleanor Erdahl, Irene Knutson, Irene Pirsig, Lila Brekke, Carolla Mosby, Esther Oppedahl

Most of our teachers were right out of college, getting some experience so they could move on to bigger schools and higher pay. One of my grade school teachers gave me a "D" in conduct. I prefer to think that the reason I got in trouble often was because my voice carried better than most.

I suppose others may remember that I have always had a big mouth! Anyway, I was afraid what my Dad would do to me when he saw the "D", but was relieved a few days later when Mother returned the card to me with Dad's signature and I could return it to my teacher. I noticed that my Dad had circled the "D" with a red pencil almost wearing a hole through the card by circling it again and again. I guessed he did that because he was upset with me and was reminding himself to be sure to discipline me for it. To my relief, he never did. When the next report card came out six weeks later, I was amazed to see that I received a "B+" in conduct. I'm only guessing, but probably that young teacher, seeing the red circles from the president of the school board, assumed the message was a threat to her rather than to me! My Dad would never have blamed a teacher for my deeds, but I always thought it turned out pretty good for me!

When I was in the eighth grade, we had a debate. The farm kids argued that the farmers could get along without the town. The town kids argued that the town could get along without the farmers. We had been waging a running argument whether the town or farms were the most important. With naive pride, I thought I had convincing arguments for the self-sufficiency of the town of Frost.

Some of the teachers were only a few years older than the students they tried to teach. One of the teachers fell in love with a senior boy and had to leave when it became obvious that they were dating. One year, we had six or eight English teachers who left before the year was over for various reasons.

A young couple who were teachers had Irish names and had attended Catholic Colleges. They even drove some distance to another community to attend a Roman Catholic Church. Imagine, practicing Catholics in our Norwegian Lutheran community! I'm not saying that we kids were narrow minded, but we considered a marriage between a Norwegian and a Swede to be a mixed marriage! I'm reluctant to admit it, but we were not at all gracious or charitable to our Catholic teachers. They may not have even been as bad at teaching as we thought. They finished the year and moved on to a friendlier place. The Lutheran Church was opposed to dancing in those days so we were not allowed to have Junior–Senior Proms. Instead, we had Junior–Senior Banquets. We had a good time but it always seemed like something was missing; the evenings ended too soon and many of us never learned how to dance.

Waitresses at the Junior–Senior Banquet, May 1953

Two of the finest teachers I had in high school shared our senior year teaching English. The first was Hazel McCarthy. She had been a college teacher and took the job in Frost to be closer to home. Her reason may have been to be with her aging parents or because she knew she had cancer and didn't have long to live. She was a wonderful teacher and inspired me to learn more about literature and to prepare for college. She grew weaker from the cancer and was forced to quit part way through the year. Her replacement was Mrs. Buchan, a younger woman, who had left teaching to become a full time wife and mother. She, too, was a wonderful teacher and a great inspiration. Pearly Hegdal, our superintendent, was also an excellent teacher. He taught chemistry, physics and a class called "Junior Business" that included basic economics and standard business practices.

I must confess that I pulled a fast one and got away with it in that class. An exam included a question that asked us to define a "negotiable instrument". I couldn't think of the correct way to respond so I wrote in "one that can be negotiated". Pearly knew me well enough to think that I knew the correct answer, so he gave me credit for my answer!

My friend and classmate, Sherwood Brekke, told me recently that Pearly Hegdal had motivated him to be a better student. He said that Pearly could have been a great preacher because he remembered so clearly all these years later how Pearly emphasized over and over that we should "take advantage of the great opportunities the taxpayers and our parents were providing in making our education possible".

Gymnasiums and Ball Fields

Our athletic facilities were limited and posed a few challenges, but then that was also true for most of our competitors. When our gym was used for sports, the stage was raised up against an end wall with a basketball hoop bolted to it.

Gymnasium with stage in raised position

When the stage was needed for a play or concert or other program such as graduation, it was lowered and draped with curtains filling almost half of the gym. The main stage curtain must have come from the old opera house. Instead of opening from the center to the sides, it was rolled up to the ceiling on a long metal pipe, probably a section of rain pipe from the hardware store with ropes at each end of the pipe. To raise the curtain, someone pulled on the ropes and it rolled up like a window curtain. More often than not, the rope slipped off the end of the pipe leaving the curtain cock–eyed and stuck until the rope could be rewound. The curtain was decorated with a scene of some kind in the center and it had small ads from various local businesses covering the rest of the canvas.

With the stage in place for a play, we had half of the gym to practice basketball (think about what a challenge that was in practicing fast breaks, etc). The drama department (the teacher in charge of plays was the department) had to schedule rehearsals and the big night during a time whenever the basketball team was playing away from home.

Our football field was on a slight hill, so we played downhill towards the north goal and uphill towards the south goal. When the field was used for baseball, the infield was always at the south end so it drained well after a rainstorm. Some of the schools we played against were in worse shape. I remember playing football in a "swamp", I think it was in Bricelyn or Kiester, where the infield was located at the low end of the field. One game in particular stands out as a real mudfest. We could barely tell anyone's number or even the color of their uniform by the end of the game. The worst thing about being a substitute player in that game was that the other subs and I were the only ones on the field with clean uniforms. Fortunately, our uniforms were as dirty as everyone else's within a few minutes if we were lucky enough to get to play at all.

Rake had a gym that was much smaller than Frost's but it had a permanent stage at one end. The edge of the stage was about a foot away from the out–of–bounds line which, in turn, was about a foot away from being directly under the basket. If you were on a fast break, you usually ended up on the stage after your shot. Fortunately, there was a thin pad covering the edge of the stage and I don't remember anyone getting hurt seriously, but it was a real challenge! The gym in Granada had a curved roof with horizontal support beams that were too low for basketball. Whenever someone threw the ball high and long (for a fast break) he would likely hit a beam and the ball would come back at him with a vengeance! Maybe the players from Granada learned how to use those beams to their advantage, but I know it was a great disadvantage to the visiting team! Delavan's gym had support posts directly behind the baskets at both ends of the court. The beams were wrapped with pads to give some protection, but they didn't help much and lots of players crashed into those posts and some probably still remember their bruises!

All the gymnasiums we played in were small by today's standards. The playing floors were narrower and shorter and none were the same size. Rake's gym was so short that the free throw circles actually overlapped the center circle! Ours was not much bigger. Small schools had a special disadvantage at tournament time. The sub district, district, regional and state tournament games were played at the larger schools and universities where the gyms were much larger, some the same size as they are today. There were no separate "classes" then, so if you were good enough to keep winning, you were matched up with much larger schools at some point in the tournament. If you had played your whole season on small gyms you were unlikely to have the stamina to run effectively up and down a gym that was half again or even twice the length and width!

Dale Hanke

Dale Hanke was our coach for basketball, football and baseball – and he also began and directed our school band, a rare combination anywhere I suspect. Dale was single the first two years he was in Frost. Then he and Donna were married and to lure Donna to Frost and keep our coach-band director, Ike Isakson built a small house just for them. It was soon after World War II and there were housing shortages everywhere, even in Frost.

When Dale and Donna Hanke moved on to their next opportunities, it took two people to replace Dale, one to coach all three sports and one to be the band director.

Orris Mortvedt is ready as Gordy Gudahl tips the jump.

George Panzram

The next coach, George Panzram, developed championship teams. We were undefeated in the regular season, one of only three undefeated teams in Minnesota for the 1949-1950 season. That team won the Border League Championship and the Sub District Tournament.

Championship team seniors. Jim Anderson, Sherwood Brekke, Ken Northwick, Dean Oswald, Al Underdahl, Neil Kittlesen

I was lucky enough to be a substitute player on that winning basketball team. One of the disadvantages of a small school is the opportunity to do things that you have little or no talent for. It does provide good lessons in humility though and it was fun to be part of a winning team. Even though I can't recall doing much to help, I guess I can say that "we" won the Border League Championship and the Sub District Tournament that year. And on a recent visit to Frost, I saw the trophy case and was proud to see my name included on those two trophies!

A year or two later, George Panzram coached an undefeated football season for Frost. George left for a better opportunity soon after but the teams went on to win more basketball titles, including the District 5 championship.

Little Frost Wins, Stays Unbeaten

Little Frost continued as one of the few undefeated high school basketball teams in the state Friday night when it registered its 14th consecutive triumph with a 49-23 decision over Delavan. Sherwood Brekke set the winning pace with 16.

MINNEAPOLIS SUNDAY TRIBUNE
March 5, 1950   S   3

ROAD TOUGHER FOR CHAMPIONS

Esko, Frost, Willmar Remain Undefeated

By TED PETERSON
Sunday Tribune Staff Writer

All eight members of last year's state high school basketball tournament field remain in the 1950 title picture as a mad scramble develops this week for 32 district championships.

The state's three undefeated teams—Eska, Frost and Willmar—swing into additional action this week.

Frost will be out to extend string of 18 in a row as it meets Sherburn in the first round of District Five at Wells Wednesday night.

Frost Still Hot, Wins 15th Tilt

Frost continued as one of the few undefeated high school basketball games in the state Tuesday night, when it defeated Huntley 51-29 for its 15th straight victory. Sherwood Brekke poured in 20 in setting the pace for Frost . . .

FROST, ESKO KEEP PERFECT BASKET SLATE

By TED PETERSON
Minneapolis Tribune Sports Writer

Frost and Esko both continued undefeated for the season, while a third of last year's state high school defending district basketball champions, Le Sueur, was deprived of its title in a busy program of eliminations Friday night.

Frost made it 18 straight as it copped the championship of a District Five subdivision at Wells by downing Kiester 37-26. Esko, with Bob Seikkula bagging 26 points after 30 the night before, rolled over Carlson 63-33 for its 20th straight win and a berth in the finals of a District 26 subdistrict at Duluth.

Frost and Esko Still Unbeaten

As the subdistrict high school basketball business fades into the final round with 10 events tonight, Frost and Esko remained undefeated and Montgomery dethroned Le Sueur, District 13 champion.

Thus Frost heads into the District Five tournament after beating Kiester 37-26 at Wells Friday night. It was the 18th straight victory for Frost.

Frost, Esko Risk Top Records

As Frost and Esko put their undefeated strings on the line, St. Paul Humboldt, defending state high school basketball champion, makes its initial bid highlighting subdistrict tournament play tonight.

Frost of District 5 seeks its 17th straight, meeting Delavan at Wells. Esko seeks No. 19 in a row, playing Floodwood in a District 26 subdistrict at Duluth.

ESKO, FROST STILL UNBEATEN

CARLTON UPSETS MARAIS QUINTET

New Ulm Debuts in 53-36 Victory

By TED PETERSON
Minneapolis Tribune Sports Writer

Esko and Frost, two of the state's three undefeated high school basketball teams, got their first taste of tournament action in Thursday night's busy schedule and both escaped unscathed.

Frost made it 17 straight in a 32-22 victory over Delavan in a subdistrict tournament of District Five at Wells. Brekker's 12 points set the pace for Frost. Kiester, a 38-30 winner over Bricelyn, will be Friday night's finals opponent for Frost.

MINNEAPOLIS MORNING TRIBUNE
Thurs., March 9, 1950 ★ 19

FROST SUFFERS FIRST DEFEAT

5 in 1949 State Tourney Triumph

By TED PETERSON
Minneapolis Tribune Sports Writer

Five of last year's state high school basketball tournament teams — Rochester, Mankato, Dawson, Brainerd, and Bemidji — all swung into Wednesday night's blistering tournament action and all pulled through unscathed.

Not so fortunate was one of the state's three undefeated teams, Frost, as that team suffered its first reverse in 19 games when it lost to Sherburn 50-45 in the first round of District Five at Wells.

ALL ROADS LEAD TO FROST

Bobby Griggs, The Music Man

Our school band was begun and directed for three or four years by Coach Hanke, then he left and Bobby Griggs arrived. Bobby Griggs, a true "music man", developed the fledgling band into a first class organization, providing a wonderful experience for the kids and the town. We had a marching band, a concert band, and band concerts at the ice cream socials between the bank and the old post office on Main Street. Bobby was a musical genius and taught the kids to love music. He brought the band and small groups to state championship ratings. He lived in Mason City, Iowa and commuted several days a week to Frost as well as having his own dance band and being on the road constantly.

Frost High School Band, 1951, Bobby Griggs at left

Bobby Griggs was born in Salem, Iowa in 1901. His father died two years later, the same year that Bobby came down with polio, leaving him fatherless and with two withered legs. His mother gave him a newspaper clipping many years later: "the wings of some are clipped so they cannot fly too high". He kept that clipping for the rest of his life and used it as a challenge to fly as high as possible in spite of his handicap. He started music lessons at age four and found music to be his lifelong passion.

Bobby attended Iowa Wesleyan College in Mount Pleasant, Iowa for two years then transferred to Ohio State University for a year, planning on a career in medicine, but music was in his heart and soul. He played with a college band and dreamed of starting a band of his own. He left Ohio State without a degree but attended summer terms at Iowa State College at Ames. Bobby started a six piece band called the "Original Iowans" and in 1932 he organized "Bobby Griggs and his Band".

BOBBY GRIGGS *and his Band*

CREATOR OF "SHAKER RHYTHM"

The most unusual idea in dance rhythm to appear in years. You won't want to miss this sensational band! (OVER)

His band became well known in Iowa, Minnesota, Wisconsin, Illinois, Missouri and South Dakota. One year, he played 17 high school proms and 40 other dances in 57 straight nights without a break. He and the band logged over 90,000 miles that year. When World War II began, he had a host of new challenges. He tried to continue playing dances, but the scarcities of gasoline, tires and everything else made that nearly impossible. Bobby was ineligible for military service because of the effects of polio, but most of his band members enlisted or were drafted. He had to find another way to express his musical talent.

Bobby was granted a wartime emergency certificate to begin teaching in Rock Falls, Iowa. At first, he taught science, history, typing and band but soon was able to move into teaching music only in Rock Falls and later Plymouth, Iowa. After a few years, in the late 40s, he arrived in Frost and the following year, added Elmore to his schedule. Now Bobby was teaching music to kids whose parents had danced to his bands of the 20's and 30's.

All of this was ten or more years before Meredith Wilson's movie, The Music Man, became such a big hit. Wilson was also from Mason City and could have been Bobby's friend since they were both musicians. Who knows, Bobby could have been the inspiration for the story!

There was no room available at the school for Bobby to have an office or a room for giving lessons. I recall having clarinet lessons sometimes in the furnace room a few feet from a noisy, hot coal furnace and boiler. Frequently, students would come into the furnace room to sneak a smoke (a good place for it since smoke was expected there). Everyone respected Bobby so they always asked him if he minded if they smoked. His usual reply was, "I don't care if you burn!" Other times we had our lessons in a cramped space under the gym bleachers, a space that was very low because there were only about four rows of bleachers above it. It was a space that was probably intended only for storage of team uniforms and chairs, etc, but it worked for lessons and nobody complained, not even Bobby, despite the extra challenge for him of getting into such tight quarters on crutches.

Bobby used his crutches so well that he amazed all of us. He was able to carry several band instruments, music, and whatever else he needed to and from his car, up and down the stairs, wherever he wanted or needed to go, and made it look like the most natural thing in the world! He had hand controls for his car to operate the accelerator, brakes and clutch. Automatic transmissions were still in the future and there were no other cars with hand controls in those days that I knew of. He could also balance himself perfectly with his crutches and swing both of his legs as if he were on a playground swing. In his early years, he even played golf, tennis, baseball, and rode a bicycle despite his handicap.

Bobby Griggs, The Music Man

The one thing Bobby didn't have was proper credentials. As superintendent, Pearly Hegdal always kept the state board of education bureaucrats satisfied by telling them that he had searched for a band leader and was unable to find a candidate with the proper degree who was willing to come to such a small town. Then a new state law was passed that would deny financial aid from the state to schools that had any teachers without accredited certificates. Bobby was "let go".

Bobby gave little thought to returning to school at that late date to earn the credentials he had foregone years earlier. He turned to parochial schools that were more interested in ability than credentials and began a new career at several schools in Iowa and Minnesota. Their gain was our loss. Frost's band was never the same. Bobby Griggs died in 1963 at the age of 62.

The School Expands

In the 1950's, Frost's population reached its peak and two major additions to the school were built. One provided a new "full size" gym with a "real" stage and more bleachers to accommodate the fans. The old gym was converted to space for a new industrial arts program and another wing was added to provide much-needed classrooms. All of the remaining country schools had been closed and consolidated with the nearby towns. As a temporary measure, several old frame one-room school buildings had been moved into Frost and placed on what had been the school playground. One of the old buildings was dubbed "Marna College" (in honor of the vanished town nearby) and housed Mrs. Hegdahl's class.

I remember working on the new construction in the summer of 1953. It was hot and hard work, mostly pushing wheelbarrows full of fresh mortar for the bricklayers. The owner of the construction company was pushing all of us hard to finish the project on time and on budget. If he felt any of us weren't moving fast enough he would take over the next wheelbarrow full of mortar and join the procession at a full run. We had two choices, run faster or get run over! I needed the money to finish my last year of college and the pay was good.

The next winter, I returned to participate in a concert on the new stage in the new gymnasium-auditorium. I was a member of the Viking Male Chorus at St Olaf College and we included Frost on our tour. It was a big night for Frost and for me. We arrived in our chartered Jefferson Lines bus and wore tuxedos for the concert. Our student director, Dale Warland, went on to direct the Macalester College Choir and The Dale Warland Singers, now internationally recognized for musical excellence. My sister Naomi was the envy of all her girlfriends when they learned that "the director of the Viking Chorus was staying at her house."

Viking Male Chorus To Appear At Frost

The Viking Male Chorus of St. Olaf College, Northfield, Minnesota, will present a concert of sacred music on Monday, April 19, at 8:15 p.m., in the Frost High School Auditorium. Admission will be: adults $1.00, students 12 years and older 50c, and under 12 years admitted free.

In 1935, on the St. Olaf College campus, a group of sprited male voices banded together under the direction of Luther Onerheim, to compose an informal musical organization that soon became popular on the hill as an energetic, expressive choir. These hardy pioneers took the name of their old-world ancestors, and so the Viking Male Chorus was begun. Onerheim was killed in the second world war, but from these humble beginnings, the Viking Chorus has continued their tradition to become one of the most famous male singing groups in the Midwest. Its unique situation, being student organized, directed, and managed, contributed to its popularity. This year's tour includes Western Minnesota, South Dakota and Iowa.

The present director of the chorus is Dale E. Warland, a senior music student from Fort Dodge, Iowa. Dale exhibits exceptional expression and control as a conductor. He has also composed a number for trumpet and men's chorus as part of this year's program. Jack Wilson, Glenwood, Minnesota, and Clinton Sathrum, Wanamingo, Minnesota, are co-business managers in charge of tour arrangements. Pre-tour highlights have included participation in the E.I.C. Evangelical Conference in Minneapolis and in the program honoring the St. Paul Winter Carnival Queen at the Coronation Pageant before an audience of 10,000 people.

The 1954 spring tour program includes sacred anthems centering about the Easter theme, as well as Negro spirituals which are always a favorite part of the program. The group has the ability to express their message with typical male gusto and enthusiasm, retaining the technical proficiency typical of all St. Olaf musical groups.

Mom and Dad

My mother was a wise and wonderful woman. I remember especially sitting near her in the kitchen and knowing that I could always talk to her about anything. She would always listen and give helpful advice without being critical or judgmental. Mom had an eighth grade education in a country school in northern Minnesota. She worked at a sorority house at the University of Minnesota and later as an upstairs maid at a University Regent's summer home on Lake Minnetonka. Mom was a classic example of a self–educated woman with an excellent command of manners, use of the language and a fine sense of style.

When Gladys Olson died suddenly at age 35, mother suggested to my brother, Jim, that he should go see Gladys' son Jimmy. Jim said that he wouldn't know what to say to his friend. Mother told him, " it doesn't matter what you say or even if you don't say anything at all. Just go and sit with him." What wonderful advice that was.

I remember staying out past dark one summer night which, of course, was forbidden. I waited by the church basement window for mother's meeting to end so I could walk home with her and escape the punishment Dad was sure to deal out. How smug I felt that I had figured out a solution! And how close I felt to mother and grateful for her love and protection.

The only time I swore in front of my mother was a memorable experience. I don't remember what word I uttered but I have never forgotten her reaction. She was washing dishes and she very calmly, without a word, filled a water glass and threw the water in my face! Then she said, "Don't **ever** use that word again!" I wish I could say that I never did use that word again, but I certainly never said it again in earshot of my mother!

As I got older, I was always selling something. I sold magazine subscriptions, newspaper delivery, mail–order seat covers for old cars (during the war and right after everyone had an old car), stamp collections, pots and pans, etc. One day a salesman came to the door and, before he could open his mouth, mother told him she wasn't interested and even if she were she would buy it from her son. He stammered, "Lady, I haven't even told you what I'm selling yet!" She replied, "It doesn't matter, if he isn't selling it now, he will be soon!"

In the summer of 1954, I worked as a salesman for Swift & Company. I worked several territories in Upper Michigan, Wisconsin, and Minnesota, covering for the regulars while they were on vacation. My brother, Jim, took a job that same summer, between his sophomore and junior years at Gustavus Adolphus College, working at a clothing store in St. Peter, Minnesota. During the week that I was based in Stillwater, Minnesota, one of the good ladies of Frost stopped Mom as she was walking down the street and asked her, "where are Neil and Jim? I haven't seen them all summer." Mother answered, "Jim is in St. Peter and Neil is in Stillwater." The lady replied, "Oh, that's too bad, they were such nice boys". For any who may need an explanation, the words St. Peter and Stillwater were synonymous at that time with the St. Peter State Mental Hospital and Stillwater State Prison. When I heard the story, I thought it might be better to be in prison than to be crazy. Jim may have had a different reaction. Mother's reaction was to see the humor and she enjoyed telling the story.

Mom and Dad were both active in church, school and community. They served on committees, held offices and were effective in getting things done. Our house was small but there was always room for guests at our dining room table. It was a round oak table with extra leaves to expand as needed and Mom could always find enough food for a few more people. Whenever Dad complained about the food bills, Mom would serve milk toast or rice with cream and sugar. Dad would then complain "when are we going to have meat around here?" and Mom had the green light to buy the groceries and meats she wanted. They remodeled the house to make room for a piano in hopes someone would learn to play it and to add the sound of music in our home. Helen has that piano in her living room today.

Nell Kittlesen, 1955

My Dad was a man of principle and integrity. He drove home one evening from a meeting in Mankato–50 miles on bad roads–so that he could vote in a local election. We have a copy of a letter he wrote to the owner of a restaurant near Brainerd. Dad thought the waitress had undercharged him one dollar and wrote that he would send the dollar if, in fact, the bill was wrong. He kept the copy with the reply thanking him and assuring him that the bill had been figured correctly. Click found the correspondence years after Dad's death and took it to the restaurant to ask if the owner remembered the story. The owner said to wait a minute, went into his office and emerged with the original letter from Dad and a copy of his reply! They were two of a kind–scrupulously honest and record keepers to boot.

No. 285

STATE BANK OF FROST

C. N. KITTLESEN, PRESIDENT
CLIFFORD KITTLESEN, VICE PRESIDENT

K. L. NESHEIM, VICE PRES. & CASHIER
DOROTHY L. NESHEIM, ASST. CASHIER

FROST, MINNESOTA

August 1st. 1960

Akre's Dutch Oven,
Cross Lake, Minn.

Gentlemen:

On Sunday evening, July 31st., I had a party of five in your place for the evening meal.

We had three steak sandwiches and two orders of 1/4th/ Fried chicken, with the regualr trimmings.

The waitress added the tab up to $7.40 and I think she short changed herself, and you. It looks to me like you should have had about $1.00 more if I remember the prices right.

Please check and let me know. If I did not pay the bill in full I will send you the balance after I get your verification.

We had a very nice time at Cross Lake and enjoyed the good meals and fine service at your place of business.

Yours very truly,

MEMBER FEDERAL DEPOSIT INSURANCE CORPORATION

Akre's Dutch Oven

Crosslake, Minnesota

KNOWN FROM COAST TO COAST

August 5, 1960

Mr. C. Kittlesen
State Bank Of Frost
Frost, Minn.

Dear Mr. Kittlesen:

Thank you for your concern about the total on your dinner check here at the Dutch Oven on July 31st.

Our menu price for the steak sandwich is $1.50 and the ½ chicken is $1.45--3X $1.50 ($4.50) 2X $1.45 ($2.90) for a total of $7.40, the amount you paid.

Thank you again for your thoughtfulness. Hope to see you next year.

                                        Sincerely,

                                        Oscar M. Akre

BAKERY   RESTAURANT   FOUNTAIN

Dad could also be stern. I remember him pulling my ear while gently but firmly booting me in the rear with the side of his foot. I learned many a lesson that way but was sure that my right ear was going to be stretched permanently in the process!

Dad also had a great sense of humor and was a master storyteller. My favorite was the one about the sale of a bull. The purchaser arrived with his horse–drawn wagon and a ramp. Unfortunately, the bull was in no mood to climb the ramp and neither the seller nor the purchaser could figure out how to coax, cajole or force the bull to climb it. Then they came up with what seemed like the perfect solution. They tied the hay sling around the bull's belly and hooked it up as if they were loading hay into the barn. The horses were supposed to pull on the rope to raise the bull just high enough so they could push the wagon underneath the bull. Then they would back the horses so that the bull would be slowly lowered into the wagon. As you might have guessed, it didn't work that way. When the bull was lifted into the air he was frightened and bellowed loudly. That scared the horses and they bolted. As they ran forward, they pulled the bull up and into the barn and when the hay sling hit the trip mechanism, the bull was dropped into the haymow. That really scared him and he charged in every direction battering his head into the walls of the barn. It was obvious that there was no way to control the bull and keep him from battering down the barn. And there was no way to reverse the hay lift–it's a one–way street. The only solution was to get the rifle and kill the bull. If you have ever seen horses load hay into a barn you can visualize this story. If you haven't and this story doesn't make sense to you, tell it to someone who farmed with horses. They'll explain it to you.

One Sunday morning Dad stood up at the end of the church service and reminded Pastor Mosby he had forgotten to call for the offering. It was one of those few times in the year when the offering was to go direct to the pastor and he either forgot or was reluctant to ask for it. I was very young and very embarrassed. How could my Dad interrupt the pastor and tell him he had forgotten? It took a while to realize that Dad had done the right thing and had helped make sure the pastor received what he was due.

My cousin, Bill Amundson wrote a wonderful memory of my Dad: "I remember Clifford so well. He would visit us in our Minneapolis flat on Columbus Avenue from time to time. He was always cheerful and sometimes, to our young eyes, a little larger than life. He was usually either on banking or checkers business, or a combination. It is his checkers interest that I will relate here. He was outstanding in that seemingly simple but extremely complicated board game. He was a recognized master and the game had been his lifelong passion. My cousin, Helen, and her husband, Roger Sather, had a friend whose heft was exceeded only by his self-regard. He constantly bragged to Roger about his accomplishments in all his endeavors. A patient man, Roger listened with his usual civility. However, even patience has its flash points. One time, when loquacious Looey, for that was his name, opined as to how he was the finest checkers player in several nearby and distant venues, Roger told him that Helen had an uncle who was a pretty good checkers player. Roger suggested setting up a game when Clifford was in town. Looey agreed, undoubtedly envisioning how he would put this small towner to shame.

"The day of the contest arrived. We all sat around our dining table to watch. It was a slaughter! Just a few moves, a very few, and large Looey was deposed. Then courtly Clifford, gracious as always, gave Looey some pointers on the game. Friendship and respect prevailed. And Roger snickered. Fast forward a few years. I was news director of a radio station in St. Louis, Missouri. One day I came across a news story reporting that a Clifford Kittlesen of Frost,

Minnesota had been winner of a national checkers competition by mail. Way to go, Uncle Clifford! But how in the world do you play checkers by mail?" It was actually a simple process. Each player had rubber stamps to make a checker board and each checker's place was marked on the board with a solid or open circle round stamp and they used penny postcards to exchange each move. It was a very slow process, but it worked well.

My sister, Naomi, recalls Dad had a beautiful flourish to his signature that was difficult to decipher, even for those of us who were very familiar with it. One of his checker correspondents was unable to read it, so he simply cut out the signature and pasted it on the address side of his postcard reply, added "Frost, Minnesota" and trusted that the post office would get it to the right person. It worked, Dad laughed about it and the game went on. And his signature seemed to be a little more legible after that episode.

When I was a senior in high school, Dad bought a new Chrysler. The production of new cars had been stopped during the war years in favor of building tanks and airplanes. I was excited to drive a 1949 luxury car instead of the old 1939 Chevrolet. My excitement vanished when Dad told me he could not afford to insure a teenaged driver for the new car. I was grounded! For life!! Or so it seemed at the time. I had little hope for buying my own car but I was desperate and went shopping. The dealer who

Clifford Kittlesen, Southern Minnesota Checkers Champion

sold Dad the new car had a 1937 Ford for sale. It was a piece of junk but to me it looked fine. The price was $100 but I could have it for $75 since my Dad was a customer. Dad insisted on looking at it before allowing me to use my own money to buy it and I was sure he was ruining the deal when he kicked the loose fenders, scowled and told the dealer, "it isn't much but I suppose we could give you $50 for it". Where did he get that "we" stuff? I choked back the words. "Clifford, this is a $100 car. I'm offering it for $75 because you're a good customer but I'm losing money on the deal" was the dealer's response. Dad kept his scowl and said, "well, if you're losing money at $75, it won't hurt you to lose a little more at $50!" The dealer's jaw dropped but he couldn't come up with an argument for that and said, "OK". So I had my first car and a good lesson on how to buy one! Paul Hegdal remembers that I got 40 acres of prime top soil and that car for only $50. It looked like it had been used in the fields for farm work. I had to take out the seats and the door panels and blast it with water from the garden hose to avoid choking on all the dust *inside* the car!

It must have been difficult to manage a bank in those days in a small community. Dad didn't own the bank so it wasn't his money at risk and he was responsible to the five or six men who did own it. He knew all the people in town and knew whether or not they would be able to repay their loans. Times were hard and people desperately needed money even when they had no realistic expectation of being able to pay it back. I remember playing basketball and being frustrated when one of my teammates refused to pass the ball to me even when I was the only one in the clear. Finally, I asked him, "Why won't you ever throw the ball to me?" He replied in anger, "Because your Dad won't give my Dad a loan!" I was stunned! Dad never talked business at home; I had no idea about such things and was glad I didn't. "What your Dad and my Dad do has nothing to do with you and me and nothing to do with how to play this game," was the only answer I could muster.

Dad was honored for completing fifty years in banking at the Minnesota Bankers Convention in Minneapolis on June 16, 1964. He would have been there if he had been in good health. He had successfully fought cancer eight years earlier and had even returned to work on a limited basis. In 1963, more cancer developed and he died at age 78 on the very day he was honored. There was a story about him in the Minneapolis paper that included the time and place for the funeral. The State Patrol posted a squad car on Main Street in front of the bank that day as a deterrent to any would-be bank robber who might have been tempted to take advantage of the situation.

Sitting Around the Radio

We used to sit on the floor around the radio listening with our ears glued to it and actually *watching* it as we listened. We would sit as close to the radio as we could crowding around it much like kids sit on the floor in front of the TV today.

We had all sorts of favorite programs: *Terry and the Pirates, Hap Harrigan, The Lone Ranger, Captain Midnight* and *Little Orphan Annie*, to name a few. These were a few of the many after-school programs designed especially for kids. In the evenings, we listened with our parents to *The Jack Benny Show, The Bob Hope Show,*

Helen and Naomi Kittlesen sitting around our RCA console radio

113

The Bing Crosby Show, Fibber McGee and Molly, George Burns and Gracie Allen, Abbott and Costello and many others. Imagination was key to enjoying radio. I can still hear (and see, in my mind's eye) the crash of cascading junk when Fibber McGee opened the closet door and everything in it piled onto the floor. Molly would tell him, "McGee, one of these days, you've got to clean out that closet!" One of my favorite radio shows was *The Lux Radio Theater,* produced and narrated by Cecil B. DeMille, and another was called *First Nighter,* a program that featured new short dramas. The latter had an opening line that went something like this: "A limousine has just arrived in front of the little theater just off Times Square. Let's see who this is. It's Mr. First Nighter! May we have a word with you sir? Can you tell us about the play you are about to see? At this point we would get a short preview of the play and then the deep-voiced announcer would dramatically continue, "As Mr. First Nighter enters the theater and takes his seat in the front row, the house lights dim and heeere's the play!"

We kids loved the radio commercials and sang them loudly in accompaniment. Even when we were playing elsewhere, we loved to repeat a line from a commercial and have a friend say the next line and so on. Do you remember the jingle that introduced *Let's Pretend* ?

> "Cream of Wheat is so good to eat, we eat it every day,
> it makes us strong as we sing this song and it makes us
> shout, HOORAY! It's good for growing children and
> grownups too to eat. For all the family's breakfast, you
> can't beat Cream of Wheat."

The fanciest radios I remember were the big floor consoles that were placed center stage in people's living rooms. Ours was an RCA with a "magic eye" that opened and closed to show visually whether you had the best possible signal. Those old radios used vacuum tubes that got very hot when the radio had been on for a while. The back of the radio was always open to provide some cooling for the tubes and that meant a regular cleaning was necessary. The tube would be layered with dust and the vacuum cleaner with a brush attachment seemed to be the best way to clean it and keep the tubes from overheating.

My nephew, Joe Nesheim, was very clever with anything electronic. He was fiddling around with one of the special wave bands on that radio one day and somehow picked up a telephone conversation between two women planning their day's activities. This was long before wireless cell phones and neither of us had any idea how the radio could pick up a telephone call. But there it was!

Not all of the radios I remember were that fancy. We had a small table model with a plastic case and photo-decals of the Dionne Quintuplets on the face of the radio. When I candled eggs at Ike's store, he had an old wooden cabinet table model radio on a shelf above the candling stations. It helped to relieve the boredom of looking at the insides of thousands of eggs although it was very old and not too reliable, which was no doubt the reason why Ike put it there. Bill Isakson and I were working together and we had a system whenever the radio cut out. Whichever of us was the fastest would take a folded egg filler (an interlocked cardboard grid to keep the eggs separated from each other on each layer of a case of 30 dozen eggs) and we would use it like a fly swatter to whack the radio and bring it back to life. It was during that time I got the idea that being a radio disk jockey would be a cool career, but then kids always dream about several careers before they hit on the one that's right for them.

A large outdoor antenna was also required to get a clear signal. At home, we had a huge "spider web" antenna that stretched between the house and a large tree. I don't suppose it was very attractive, but it did bring a clear signal on the standard broadcast band as well as short wave, long wave, ultra short and, if I remember right, about a half dozen different bands of broadcasts from all over the world.

There were fewer radio stations then and at night, when the daylight only stations went off the air, we could always pick up the 50,000-watt clear channel stations from Pittsburgh and New Orleans and sometimes even foreign broadcasts. I remember hearing Adolph Hitler's hysterical ranting and raving and the calm, deliberate, reassuring and inspiring words of Winston Churchill.

Another distance broadcast came from a semi-legitimate station in Del Rio Texas that used a broadcast tower located across the border in Mexico to avoid FCC regulation and enable them to drown-out any smaller station with a wavelength that was close.

On Saturday mornings, we listened to *Grand Central Station*. I can still hear the announcer beginning the show with (the words as I remember them):

> "Like a speeding bullet seeks its target, shining rails from every part of this great country point towards New York City. Drawn by the magnetic force of this fantastic metropolis, day and night great trains rush toward the Hudson River, sweep down its eastern bank for a hundred and forty miles, dive with a roar into the three and a half mile tunnel that burrows beneath the glitter and swank of Park Avenue, and then "Grand Central Station", crossroads of a million private lives, gigantic stage on which are played a thousand dramas daily".

We spend a lot of time in airline terminals these days as we enjoy our retirement traveling – visiting family and friends and sightseeing around the country and around the world. I remember that dramatic Grand Central Station introduction and it makes me think about the thousands of dramas played out daily in airline terminals as people travel for pleasure and business; dramas of reunion and separation, joy and sorrow, peace and pain.

Flying

In the summer of 1935, a barnstorming pilot landed in a pasture on the edge of Frost and offered rides to anyone with 75 cents and enough nerve to fly in an open cockpit biplane. I was only 3 years old and didn't even hear about this great civic event until much later. My brother Jim was about six and wanted to fly so he asked Dad for 75 cents. Dad pointed at the rickety-looking frail craft circling above and told Jim; "No child of mine will ever fly in one of those things! " (Has every parent who ever lived uttered the words "No child of mine will ever _____ at least once?)

What he didn't know until later was that our brother John was in the plane he was pointing at! John had his own 75 cents and knew better than to ask permission. I would have never heard this story except for my curiosity years later wondering how Jim and I had persuaded Dad to let us fly at an air show in Austin in 1939 when I was only six. Aviation was very young back then, Lindbergh had crossed the Atlantic alone only 12 years earlier. Dad must have decided by then that it was no use trying to hold back progress or the dreams of small boys! Jim and I had our first plane ride in a Stinson, like the one in this photo.

1937 Stinson SR-10G

From that day forward I was hooked on flying. When I was about 12 years old I started saving money from my various jobs and sales to add to my flying experiences.

Whenever I had $3.00 saved up I would ride my bike or catch a ride to the Blue Earth airport where I could buy a 20 minute ride for $3.00. My dream was to take flying lessons as soon as I had the money for it and to solo at age 15, the earliest legal age for it in those days. Lack of enough money and the realization that I had better save what I could for college put that dream on the back burner but I did get many $3.00 rides and have always enjoyed flying.

As a kid I remember hearing a story one day in Bergo's Café about two fellows who owned an open cockpit biplane. They were flying one day and each thought the other was in command and that they were the passenger. The plane crashed into a tree leaving them shaken but luckily unhurt. It left an indelible impression on me that you should always know who's in command and you need to take charge when it's your turn!

During the war years we saw many bombers flying over Frost on their way to Minneapolis to be fitted with precision bomb sights before going on to the Pacific or European war zones. The bombers were an awesome sight. We had air raid drills and dutifully covered all our windows with black shades. I remember memorizing silhouettes of every friendly and enemy airplane in service during World War II. If any enemy planes had attacked Frost, I was ready.

Outhouses and Halloween

In the 1930's and 1940's, indoor plumbing was becoming more common and it would be a stretch to call it a luxury. But there were many people who still used an outhouse and many more who still had them on their property even though they had added bathrooms with all the facilities. So outhouses were a common sight and since they were not all being used on a regular basis, they seemed to be fair game for Halloween pranksters.

Tipping outhouses on Halloween was not as hard as you might think. If the outhouse was old, as most of them were, the wood around the base was beginning to rot and some didn't even have any built-in protection against the little monsters of Halloween. All it usually took was two or three kids giving a push together and over it went. Tipping it back up again and placing it just behind the hole was about the worst trick of all. If it was in a dark area, as most of them were, all you had to do was hide and wait for the next group of kids to spot it and run towards it to tip it. Once I remember a friend falling into the hole. I won't even try to tell you what a rotten trick that was!

There was at least one family that used their outhouse to store their storm windows during the "off-season". Since it was a good idea to get ready for winter early, the storm windows were always out of the outhouse before Halloween. One year we had exceptionally warm and even hot weather late into the fall. Since no one had air conditioning in those days you certainly wanted to open your windows to cool off and it would have been ridiculous to have storm windows on in such warm weather. Unfortunately, one family forgot that their storm windows were still in the outhouse on Halloween. As you might expect, someone chose that particular outhouse for tipping that year. The crash of breaking glass was deafening! I couldn't tell you who any of those kids were but I can assure you that no one took "credit" for tipping that outhouse!

When we were kids Halloween meant license for mischief and there were few limits on what was acceptable and what was not. Soaping windows may have been a more excusable trick in mild weather but, if it turned cold and stayed cold, the victims of that prank might have to put up with soaped windows for an entire winter. Another common trick was to "steal" and hide anything left outside. The bench in front of Leonard's Café usually could be found on the roof of the bank the day after. You learned quickly to put everything away before dark on Halloween. If you forgot, you might spend days looking for your hoses, lawn chairs, garden tools and even your garbage can!

A few years ago, on impulse, I told a kid at my door that I didn't have any treats and he would just have to trick me. He gave me a look that told me he didn't have a clue about doing a trick. So I just smiled and said I was kidding and gave him some candy. He went on his way and probably told his friends about the weird guy who wanted a trick. We had a lot of fun on Halloween when we were kids but, as an adult, I have to admit that "trick or treat" is a much better idea!

Outhouses came in many sizes. Most were small with two holes but I remember my grandparents had one that you might call the "large family economy model". It had three holes across the back bench for adults and two more on a lower bench for the children. We saw one in a pioneer village in Sweden a few years ago that had seven holes placed along a semi-circular bench. Now that must have been either for a very large family or maybe it was a community social center!

Building an outhouse was not as simple as you might think. If you built it with the door facing south, you could leave the door partly open and catch the sun and fresh air. If you dug the pit deep, you would not have to dig again for a long, long time. Toilet tissue was considered a luxury and many folks made do with the pages of an old Sears Roebuck catalog. A few hardy souls felt that corncobs would do just fine. If you built the outhouse near the woodpile, you could more easily bring in a few logs after each visit and keep the wood box full without much extra effort. Should you ever run out of things to be grateful for, you can always thank God for plumbing!

When Frost appointed a young man still in his teens to be the town cop, there were a lot of people who dreaded the next Halloween. They all knew that this young man had been very creative with outrageous trickery every year since he had been old enough to tip his first outhouse. Well, everyone was in for an unexpected surprise. He rounded up several of his buddies who had been partners in Halloween destruction and deputized them! He and his deputies knew every trick in the book and who, when, where and what to be on the lookout for. They put a lid on that Halloween and it must hold the record for the quietest and most peaceful year ever!

Paper Boy

I became the paperboy for the town of Frost at age 11, one year younger than the "required age". It was a great experience. I was responsible for prompt delivery and for collecting payment from my customers so I was billed for the cost of the papers delivered to me and my profit consisted of the difference. If I didn't collect from every customer every week, I still had to make my payment to the company. It was good training in how to run any kind of business. Most of my customers were very good about having the amount due ready for me when I got to their house. Dr. Hanson always paid several weeks in advance so that I wouldn't be short if he was away caring for a patient.

My limited ability with the Norwegian language was evident when I tried to collect from Chris Anderson and his wife, Tillie. They always insisted that I ask for the amount due in Norwegian. When they just took the daily paper, it was "fem og tjue sent" (25 cents). When I convinced them to take the Sunday paper also, I wished I hadn't. The new amount was "sju og tretti" (37 cents) for a full week's service and that was too hard for me to remember—and to pronounce. When Mom and Dad bought a new sofa and chair for our living room, Jim and I were given the chance to sell the old sofa and keep whatever we got for it. Chris and Tillie bought it from us for $10, a good deal for them and for us!

I was delivering my paper route when I heard the sad news that Roosevelt died and the wonderful news that World War II was over. The fire siren was used to announce important events (and 12 o'clock noon). When the fire siren announced the good news, I had just dropped the paper in the door for Tillie Anderson. She stopped me and asked why the siren was blowing. I told her that the war was over. She said "Thank God." I suppose almost everyone said the same thing when they heard but I remember hearing her response as clearly as if it had happened yesterday.

When I had the paper route the big incentive was to win the annual trip to Minneapolis by getting a certain number of new subscribers. It was tough because I already had most of the people in town on my route but I did win several trips. A tour of the Star Tribune publishing plant was always included and sometimes a University of Minnesota Golden Gophers football game. Once, about 1947, we were treated to a tour of KSTP's new television studio where we were each to appear *on television!* That was pretty disappointing! We were herded into a makeshift trailer and told to look to the left for a quick glimpse of our faces in the TV monitor. Big deal!

Along with all the good memories about my paper route there were embarrassing moments too. Once I was so excited about being invited to go to Blue Earth with a friend to see a movie that I completely forgot to deliver my papers or even to find a substitute. As soon as we got to Blue Earth I called home and asked my sister, Naomi, to be my substitute. Another time a friend went with me on the route one evening and thought it would be fun to put rocks and sticks between the doors along with the papers. I remember we thought it was a good joke until I realized later that night that I would have to collect from everyone in a couple of days. Later, when I came to Leo Maland's house, he opened the door and invited me to step inside while he went to the next room to get the money for me. While he was gone I stood in the entry looking at the large tree branch we had put in his door. I couldn't think of anything to say and was greatly relieved when he paid me without saying anything about the branch. As I was trying to leave as fast as I could he asked in a very kind way, "Aren't you forgetting something, Neil?" It left a lasting impression on me about the consequences of doing something stupid.

I was the paperboy for Frost for five years and had a driver's license the last year. My brother, Click, was home from the war and was always out very late on Saturday nights. The Sunday papers were very heavy to carry so I worked out a pretty good system. When I got up to start my route Click was deep in the land of dreams. I would ask him if he minded if I used his car. He always answered with a "Ummnn." Then I would ask where the keys were and he again would answer "Ummnn." I took that to mean it was OK and my job was much easier on those mornings!

As the paperboy I knew the names of everyone who lived in Frost. I could take a tour of the town mentally and list the adults and kids in every house, up and down each block. I can't recall them all now, but the map of Frost in the front of this book includes as many family names and homes as best I remember them.

The News from Frost

Frost had a newspaper, The Frost Record, from 1899 to 1919, but I didn't know about it until I started doing research for this book. While I was growing up Frost had a small section in the *Faribault County Register* and the *Bricelyn Sentinel*. The typical items in those sections would be something like "Mr. and Mrs. Clifford Kittlesen were visitors for dinner at the home of Mr. and Mrs. Ed Bartel last Tuesday evening." Jim Johnson, a friend who grew up in Bricelyn, gave me the following stories that appeared in the "Looking back in the old files" section of the *Bricelyn Sentinel*:

Fifty Years Ago

Frost—Neil Kittlesen and Kermeth Northwick are co-valedictorians and Kenneth Northwick is the salutatorian of the 1950 senior class. Other class members are James Anderson, Sherwood Brekke, Evelyn Clark, Richard Fenske, Thelma Nodland, Dean Oswald, Barbara Thompson and Alfred Underdahl.

Forty Years Ago

Frost—"On June 7,(1954) the 26th wedding anniversary of Mr. and Mrs. C. Kittlesen, their son, Neil, received his bachelor of arts degree from St. Olaf College in Northfield. The Kittlesens also entertained a number of guests through the week in honor of Naomi's graduation from high school and Helen's confirmation."

The local papers were so different from the Minneapolis papers that they might have come from different worlds. In a sense, I guess they did. We read them all because we were part of both worlds. When my sister, Dorothy, and her husband, Kenny Nesheim, lived in Rake I would often see their paper, the *Rake Register*. Underneath the masthead every copy proudly proclaimed: "The Only Newspaper in the World Interested in Rake." Speaking of Rake, did you hear this one? Question: "where are you going?" Answer: "to Rake." Question: "rake what?" Answer: "Rake, Iowa." Question: "all of it?"

People

The farmers and townspeople of Frost were almost all Norwegian immigrants but we also had Indian John (actually a Mexican according to my brother Jim) who hauled garbage to the town dump for people willing to pay and unwilling to do it themselves. My sister Naomi tells me that one of her friends was in Indian John's house and saw discarded photos that John had retrieved from the trash and displayed as "his" family.

I remember the first black man I ever saw. He was one of many itinerants who came through during the depression. He may have been a preacher but I don't remember for sure.

There were peddlers, scissors sharpeners and hobos. Most of the hobos caught rides on the freight trains from town to town, camped out near the tracks and were an attraction for small boys who had the nerve to go talk with them. One, calling himself Hairbreadth Harry, was a poet. I can still remember one of his poems:

> Hairbreadth Harry is no fairy
> He can neither flit nor float nor fly
> But he is like you and I
> He must eat or he will die.

His poem was very effective; we all ran home to our mothers to beg for sandwiches for him. Hobos were also called bums, tramps or beggars. The term "hobo" actually is a contraction for "homeward bound" and referred to the many civil war veterans who were told to find their own way home when the war ended. Most started out for home by catching a ride on a train by crawling into an empty boxcar. Most of those who were homeward bound couldn't wait to see their loved ones again and got home as soon as they could. A few developed a liking for seeing the country with free rides and the carefree life after the horror of war and never did return home. They continued to "ride the rails" and begged for food wherever they found someone sympathetic and slept on the trains or near the tracks. As the years passed and it became obvious to all that they were no longer "homeward bound", the term shortened into "hobo."

Ole Hattlestad, a house painter, didn't use a drop cloth in his work. He never spilled a drop of paint because, as he put it, "paint costs money." Juhl Wilmert found it hard to believe that anyone could paint without ever spilling occasionally and he insisted that Ole use a drop cloth before he would hire him to paint the front of his Red & White grocery store. Ole reluctantly bought a drop cloth at Ted Gullord's hardware store with the provision that he could bring it back for a full refund if it didn't have a single drop of paint on it. He finished the job without spilling a drop and got his refund. Ole was a bachelor with a small coupe. One day, two spinsters from Frost needed a ride to the church at Dell so Ole offered them a ride. When they got into the car, the skirt of the lady sitting in the middle inadvertently covered the floor shift lever. Ole was too shy to say anything and fortunately the gears were in the forward second position, so he drove the four miles to Dell in second gear.

John Bones lived on a farm a few miles west of Frost. I remember seeing him walking along the gravel road near his farm as we drove by. He had a very long beard and was a scary person for a young boy. His house and all of the buildings on his farm had lost whatever paint they ever had. The roofs were collapsing and it looked like the stereotypical haunted house. The explanation for all of this seemed to be that his father had made all of the decisions and after his death John was terrified to do anything that might change the way the place looked, living in fear that his dead father would return and punish him for changing things. Obviously he couldn't see the decay from one day to the next. A sad story and a scary place.

One of the upstanding women of Frost objected to wine being served at some function. She was reminded that Jesus converted water to wine at the wedding in Cana. "Well, I think he could have left that out," was her quick response.

A woman who lived near the school had a fine apple tree that was her pride and a great temptation to many kids. Some were clever enough to convince her they only took apples that had fallen to the ground. Some adults, including my Mom, were upset when she offered them apples and after they had accepted told them they owed her money. Well, times were hard and she was probably trying to make ends meet like everyone else.

We had a unique group of people who were known by colorful nicknames; Termite, Dutch, Blacky, Whitey, Dynamite, Lightning, Puna, Poop, Uffda, Tupin, Click and Soualeecha. Termite was, as you might guess, very short for her age. Blacky and Whitey were cousins with the same names but one had coal black hair and the other had white tow-headed hair. Dynamite and Lightning were brothers with a talent for daring outrageous acts from the time they were toddlers. When Lightning was three years old, he was called Firecracker because he was slightly less volatile than his brother but he soon outgrew that name! It's hard to imagine the whole town calling a kid "Poop" but that's what he was called. Uffda used that wonderful Norwegian catch-all expression so often that it became her nickname. Tupin wore two pairs of pants, one over the other, to keep warm in the winter and Two-Pants became Tupin. My brother was known as Click for as long as I remember, but I have no idea where his nickname came from. Soualeecha didn't bathe and had a strong odor that was too much for everyone including his friends. They got him drunk once and took him to the creek and gave him a good scrubbing with lots of soap and coarse brushes. His strange nickname might mean something in Norwegian but it is as much a mystery as why creeks were known as "cricks".

When everyone knows everyone as they do in small towns, you grow up within a refreshing atmosphere of honesty and straight talk. I was in another small town a few years ago. While in a restaurant I heard a conversation between the waitress and a customer, "Hey, Emil, I hear you sold your house." He quickly replied, "Ain't seen no money yet!" Well, I guess if you ain't been paid you ain't sold it yet!

The Ski Hill

If you grew up in Frost, you had a different idea about what a hill looks like. The land is about the richest soil you can find on earth and it is also the flattest, both of which are good for farming. We did have a hill on the golf course two miles east of town that served as a pretty good hill for skiing. I remember we made ski jumps by packing mounds of snow on the slope and it took a lot of nerve to ski down that hill whether we went over the jump or not.

Twelve years ago, I took my wife, Bobbie, to Frost for the annual dinner theater. We arrived early, so after a quick tour around town, I thought it would be fun to show her our ski hill. Now Bobbie spent some of her growing up years in Washington State between the Olympic Mountains and the Cascades, so I wasn't sure what she would think of "our ski hill." When we got there, I was amazed to see that the hill was gone! "Someone must have moved it," I commented in disappointment. All we could see was a slight rise in an open field. Then it dawned on me! It was, in fact, just as it had been when I was growing up! Of course, I was much smaller then and I had yet to see any real hills or mountains.

Smaller than Frost

Dell had more to offer than the church and parsonage but not much more. It had an elementary school and a general store run by the Schanke brothers. Their store had a little bit of just about everything buried under tons of junk. It looked like it had never been cleaned since the day it was built. To get to the ice cream freezer you had to remove several layers of stuff that was parked on top of it. One day a customer complained that the oatmeal she bought there had a strange taste "like maybe there were mice in the barrel." "Oh, that's not possible, Missus, the cat gave birth to kittens in that barrel so there couldn't be any mice in there!" I don't remember when it closed but antique lovers would have a field day there if it still existed.

Another small town we all called "Podunk." It had a store, gas station, and a cafe and was on Highway 16 just a short ways east of the Frost corner. I remember wondering why the sign on the highway named it Brush Creek and learned much later that many small towns were called "Podunk."

I remember another one-time town that we called Pineapple Junction but I can't remember where it was. It seems to me that it was just a crossroads with a foundation or two from buildings that had vanished and was within a few miles of Frost.

Epilogue

Frost was a self-sufficient community in those days. We had churches and a school. We had a general store and another store providing competition for groceries. We had a meat market and smokehouse to provide locally made hams, bacon and sausage as well as fresh meat from local farms. We had two grain elevators, a dairy and a creamery. We exported our farmers' excess grain, sugar beets, butter and eggs. We had a railroad and trucking line or two to provide the shipping. We had a hardware store. We also had a blacksmith shop and a harness shop when they were needed for the horses used in farming. We had several gas stations—at least three at the same time, maybe four. We had our own locally–owned telephone company, a bank and a post office that served the community and provided rural mail delivery. We had at least three restaurants at any one time. We had a lumberyard. We had coal delivery at a time when many people heated their homes with coal. We had a pool hall, ice skating rink and free movies for entertainment. We had town teams providing baseball and softball games on weekends. Some of the town teams were pretty good. We also had visiting Negro League teams with some outstanding players (Blacks were not allowed on major league teams back then). The migrant workers had some great players too and listening to their banter in a foreign language added to our education. It was a nice clean community with good people who cared about and for each other.

There were also things Frost didn't have. A small school with small classes couldn't compete with the offerings and experienced teachers of larger schools. We didn't have any paved roads in Frost or leading to Frost until the early 1950's. We didn't have a single block with sidewalks on all four sides (but then we only had about six blocks with buildings on four sides). We didn't have a drug store but Doc Hanson provided whatever medicines he prescribed and the grocery stores offered all the non-prescription drugs and other merchandise we associate with drug stores. We didn't have a furniture store. We didn't have a movie theater, bowling alley or a roller skating rink during my growing up years.

The things we didn't have were all available to us within about 15 to 30 miles. But when the roads were poor that was too great a distance for everyday travel. When the roads were paved and bigger stores were built in the larger towns, it was no longer necessary or desirable to do all your shopping so close to home. As farmers began to use more sophisticated equipment and specialized more, they no longer needed as many workers or the services small towns offered. Better opportunities were to be found in the larger cities, as a result more and more of the children left and the town began to decline.

What is the future for small towns like Frost? Some small towns are finding new purposes–new businesses, tourism, becoming bedroom communities, etc. People like me who have left their small towns probably don't have the right to even suggest solutions. Perhaps the question can best be answered by those who still live in Frost and other small towns. Their creativity and imagination will find the answers for the towns that do survive and prosper in the new millennium.

The End

Neil Palmer Kittlesen lived in Frost from birth to high school graduation. He is a 1954 graduate of St Olaf College and served in the US Army in Orleans, France in 1955-1956.

He recently retired after 40 years in the insurance and investment industry. From 1977 to 1988, Neil was the General Agent for Lutheran Brotherhood in Mankato serving south central Minnesota, including Frost.

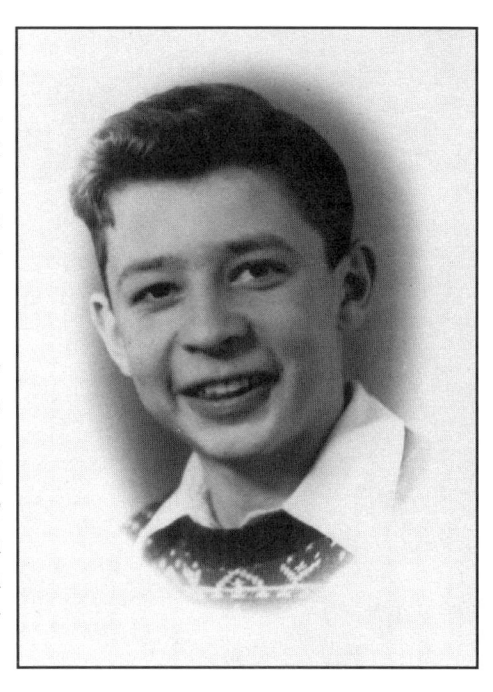

Widowed twice, Neil married Barbara (Bobbie) Spradley in 1988. They have seven married children and sixteen grandchildren. Neil and Bobbie share interests in writing, travel, photography and family history.